CLASSIC MOTORING
FROM
PUNCH

Designed and produced by Parke Sutton Publishing Limited, Norwich
for the Publishing Division of The Automobile Association, Basingstoke.

Editor Paula Granados

Designer Geoff Staff

Typesetting by P.S. Typesetting, Lowestoft.
Colour origination by Blackfriars Colour Repro, Norwich.
Printed and bound by Cronion S.A., Barcelona, Spain.

A CIP catalogue record for this book is available from the British Library.

Published by The Automobile Association,
Fanum House, Basingstoke, Hampshire RG21 2EA

ISBN 0 7495 0399 8

CONTENTS

INTRODUCTION   4

INTRODUCTION

Imagine life without the motor car. No furry dice, no Tufty Club, nothing for AA men to salute, nothing to do on the M25, nothing to clean on Sunday mornings, nothing for Murray Walker to do on Sunday afternoons. When Gottlieb Daimler skipped out of his workshop in 1883, smelling slightly of petrol, he had not just invented a new engine, he had invented a completely new way of life. And with a new way of life, came a new strand of humour.

Motorists and motoring have provided writers and cartoonists with endless material. And early motorists were such easy targets. What could be more ridiculous than a man with a red flag strutting about the countryside on a lazy Victorian afternoon followed by a carload of England's finest, peering through goggles and bracing themselves against speeds of up to 12 mph.

Trust the French to get jealous, though. For nearly 30 years, the French smarted at all the fun we seemed to be having across the Channel. Early motoring seemed designed for the British. Only we could show such devoted interest in the development of the synchromesh gear change with silent second facility. Only we would find it exciting to slip into a garish tweed hat, thick goggles and warm cape for a 10 mph trip to the coast, probably involving two breakdowns and treatment for frostbite.

It took an idea of outstanding eccentricity to kickstart the French motor industry into life. And in 1935, Pierre Boulanger, of Citroën, had that idea. 'Make me a car', he told his designers, 'in which a farmer wearing a top hat can carry a 110lb sack of potatoes across a ploughed field without bumping his head on the roof'. They should have said 'Push off, matey,' but he was the boss, so they said 'Straight away, monsieur' instead and came back days later with the Citroën 2CV – one headlamp, one colour, 0-60 in three weeks, and a bump in the roof big enough to accommodate the largest in French agricultural headgear. Yes, those were the days.

Motoring just doesn't seem as much fun any more. Where motor manufacturers once boasted that their cars could reach 60 mph before you shut the door properly, now they tell us how you can rock a baby to sleep in the back and have the chassis recycled in time for the child's 21st. We feel guilty about our exhaust fumes, about excess oil, about how much petrol we use, or if we're over the limit. And if we're not feeling guilty, we're cross about how much traffic there is on the road, and about how badly everybody else drives.

This book is a reminder of when people used to enjoy motoring, the days before the radar gun, before the breathalyser, before the Hanger Lane gyratory system, the days when you could buy the very latest in farm vehicle technology, and still have cash to spare for a top hat and a sack of potatoes.

ROLAND WHITE
PUNCH

THE THREE-LITRE BENTLEY
Guaranteed 5 years
Fuel consumption 25 m.p.g.
Chassis Price. £875

BENTLEY MOTORS LTD.
3 HANOVER COURT, LONDON W1

THE PERSONAL ELEMENT AT A MOTOR SHOW

NOT to be outdone by Olympia we have just held a motor show in our provincial Town Hall. What though the motoring magazines, obese with the rich diet of advertisement, grew no fatter in its honour, it was at least the most successful social function we have known since the War began. The Town Hall externally was magnificent with flags by day and coloured lamps by night, and within was a blaze of bunting and greenstuff. The band of the Free Shepherds played popular music, and the luncheon and tea rooms were the scene of most delightful little gatherings. Besides all this, quite a number of cars were to be found amongst the decorations.

Nearly every demobilised officer in the county seems to have taken up an agency for a car or two, and bought himself spats on the strength of a prospective fortune. Jimmy Wrigley and I are amongst them. Wrigley in the Great War was M.T., R.A.S.C., and knows so much about cars that he can tell the make of lamps from the track of the tyres; while I was a cavalryman and know so little that I judge Jimmy's cleverness only by other people's incredulity. On our stand at the show we exhibited two cars, which, as I carefully learned beforehand from the book of the words, were a Byng-Beatty and a Tanglefoot, these being the cars for which we are what they call concessionaires. (The *bât* is tricky, but one picks it up loafing about garages.)

As a rule Jimmy and I do the correspondence between us—Jimmy contributing the technique and I the punctuation; but for the three days of the show his cousin Sheila volunteered to preside at a dainty little table and make jottings of our orders. Sheila is always ornamental, and as we had the stand draped to tone with her hair, and she wore a dress which harmonized like soft music with the pale heliotrope of the Tanglefoot's body-work, our display was a magnet from the word "Go".

And then on the morning of the opening day Jimmy went down with his Lake Doiran malaria and left me to it!

I am as brave as most people, but this calamity unmanned me. "Sheila," I said to a pair of pitying grey eyes, as the crowd, having heard the show declared open, massed about our stand—"Sheila, the situation is desperate. These people will ask me about the cars. They will expect me to answer them intelligently, and it's no use in the world talking horse to them—I can see that from their sordid looks. I shall disappear. You can say I have gone out on a trial run, which won't be a lie, only an understatement. And you can just hand them out the little books and let them paw the varnish. Silence will be better than anything I could say. Probably it is better than what any conscientious man could say about the Tanglefoot."

"I'll carry on, Nobby," said Sheila. "You go and buy buns for Miss Hurdlewing, and be happy. Fly! here's a purchaser."

Sheila's whisper dispersed me into the crowd and I strolled away, while she bestowed a smile and a specification pamphlet on the first of the crowd to step on to our stand.

I found it impossible to keep away for long. Sheila looked so well against the heliotrope Tanglefoot limousine that I had to go back to look at her.

The stand was surrounded by a throng, hushed and breathless with interest. Sheila was talking volubly. Hardened motorists listened with their mouths open; zealots, feverish to expend their excess profits on motoring because it was a novelty and expensive, stood spellbound; a rival agent drank in her words with tears in his eyes—tears for his old innocence—and his cheek flushed with a sudden and splendid determination to amalgamate with our firm.

"This chassis, gentlemen," Sheila was saying, with a glance towards the Byng-Beatty, "has the most exclusive features. The torque-tube being fitted with an automatic lighter, it is possible to change tyres without leaving your seat; while by a simple adjustment of the universal joint the car will take any reasonable obstacle gracefully and without any inconvenience to the occupants. The clutch is of the Alabama type. This new pattern created a great sensation at Olympia, owing to the ease with which it permits even the amateur driver to convert the present body into a *char-à-banc* or a tipping-waggon. The hood is reversible, so that passengers may be sheltered from the wind when the car runs backwards. In the rear of the boot, concealed by a door flush with the panels, is an EINSTEIN parachute, by means of which a passenger may leave the car before an imminent accident or when tired of the company."

I could not move; I did not want to either; and I certainly dared not interrupt.

"The Tanglefoot," continued Sheila, while a sigh of sheer rapture rose from the crowd, "is pre-eminently the car for a medical man or pushful undertaker. No horn is supplied, though this will be fitted if desired. The car is not cheap, but properly used will soon repay itself. Amongst the accessories supplied with the standard chassis I should like to call your attention to the collapsible game-bag and landing-net."

This went on for a long, long time, and I stayed till a man in the crowd recognised me and showed symptoms of coming out of his trance. I fled, and returned only at the luncheon interval.

"Sheila," I said—"Sheila, this may be fun for you, but James Wrigley and I may sing in the streets to pay for it."

"You great stupid"—her eyes were sparking as she spoke—"I've booked more orders than you will be able to carry out before you've learned wisdom. Look!" It was practically a nominal roll of the local capitalists that she showed me. "Nobody believes what you say about a car, so you can say what you like. The thing is to get it noticed."

"Did they study these cars much before they let you take their names?"

Sheila looked into my eyes and laughed happily.

DEALER. "There's a real bargain for you, Sir. She'll still do her thirty-five, and twenty to the gallon, although she's pre-war."
PROSPECTIVE PURCHASER. "Which one?"
DEALER. "This one, Sir—with the hood up."
PROSPECTIVE PURCHASER. "Yes—I see. I meant which war?"

1920

The All **Standard** British Light Cars

Specially designed for the Owner Driver

His Standard *of* Comfort
Economy, Efficiency,
Ample Power & Easy Control

*Send your name and
address for full particulars.*

The Standard Motor Co., Ltd., Coventry.

London Showrooms: 49, Pall Mall, S,W,1.

1924

Carefree Days

IF you want your car to give you real
pleasure it is only fair that you should
give it real lubrication—the grade of
Gargoyle Mobiloil specified in the Chart
of Recommendations.

Wherever you go you can obtain Gargoyle
Mobiloil and ensure perfect running and
carefree days

"*Correct Lubrication*" is an interesting
and well-illustrated booklet upon this important subject. Write for a copy to-day.

Mobiloil
Make the Chart your Guide

Head Office: Caxton House, S.W. 1

VACUUM OIL COMPANY, LD

1923

A TRAFFIC TANGLE

"YOU'll pardon me," suddenly remarked the old gentleman in the corner of the third-class smoker as he laid down his paper and cut into the conversation which had been in progress between his two fellow-travellers ever since they had got in at Woking, "but I've just been reading an article about the motor-traffic in the London streets; and from what I could not help overhearing of your discussion I gather that both of you are drivers of motor-vehicles."

The two men looked round and stopped their talk, which was highly technical and ran on such mysteries as magnetos and throttle-valves. The old gentleman was obviously right; for, though there was about the smaller of the pair a dapper alertness that suggested the ex-soldier, and the burly breeziness of his companion betrayed a former professional acquaintance with blue water, it was evident that the present vocation of both was the driving of motors.

"Now," continued the old gentleman, "it would interest me extremely to hear the opinions of such practical authorities as yourselves upon this difficult question—that is, of course, if you possess, as I surmise, actual experience of driving in the metropolitan area."

"Never driven nowhere else," said the smaller man, with a touch of barrack-room curtness and a significant glance at his *confrère*.

"Capital!" chortled the old gentleman, rubbing his hands and moving relentlessly nearer to his victims; for his chattiness, pent-up since Basingstoke, had been raging within him for an opportunity of release. "You see," he went on, "I'm just an ordinary member of the public. I can't afford to keep a car or to take taxis very often, so that I seldom get a chance of hearing the matter discussed from the driver's point of view. And omnibus-drivers are strangely uncommunicative! It's embarrassing to try to talk to them from the inside, and if before getting in or after alighting one ventures to address a few words to them from the kerb, they seem to be a little short—"

"They ain't got much time for chattin'," said the ex-soldier, "not with the timekeeper glarin' at 'em from the pavement an' clockin' the poor blokes to the umpteenth of a second."

"Quite so. Precisely. That's my difficulty," purred the old gentleman, warming to his work; "so now that I can seize the occasion of talking uninterruptedly with two such experienced—er—practitioners as you appear to be, I'm confident that you'll give me the benefit of your—er—tested knowledge on one or two salient points. First, as regards the control of traffic by the police. Do you find that you're often held up unnecessarily by the constables on point-duty?" and, adjusting his horn-rimmed spectacles on the very tip of his nose, he peered at his companions with the air of a K.C. worrying a witness.

"Carn't say as I do," answered the big ex-bluejacket, resigned by now to the inevitable. "'Course I've got lots o' pals in the Force, an' I considers it their duty to watch-out for *me*. I don't waste much time in thinking about the coppers. But I've nothing to complain of about 'em. They stops everything else for me, and—"

"One moment!" exclaimed the old gentleman with sudden ferocity; "do you mean to tell me, Sir, that the police allow private friendship to interfere with their public duty? that they let you through when they stop others because—"

"Dunno 'bout friendship," cut in the big man coolly, "but I whizzes past 'em right enough, an', if one of 'em was to try an' 'old *me* up, I reckon 'e'd soon find 'isself on the bloomin' carpet."

"Do you mean to say, Sir," thundered his astonished questioner, "that police constables are terrorised into this iniquitous favouritism?"

"Dunno 'bout terrorisin'," was the reply; "but, if one of 'em was to stand in the road in front o' *my* scarlet-runner, well, 'e wouldn't live long enough to worry about bein' terrorised."

"But this is astounding. Paris is nothing to it!" gasped the old gentleman, now quite purple in the face, as he turned to the little ex-soldier. "And you, Sir—May I ask whether *you* endorse such monstrous and anti-social partiality?"

"Well, I sorter works with the pleece, you see, Sir," said the little man mildly; "they always lets *me* through, even when the traffic's stopped for Royal percessions an' suchlike. Allowin' for the difference in pace, it's much the same with me as with Jim 'ere. There ain't no 'urry for *me* an' my ole 'bus; I jus' trundles along quite 'appy at about ten miles p.h., an' never stops for no one."

"Gobbless my soul, but this is amazing!" choked the old gentleman, breathless with bewilderment. "'Never stops for no one!' And what about your passengers, may I ask? I can understand their pleasure at not being 'held up'; but suppose they want to get out? Is there no bell in your 'bus, Sir?"

"I never stops to ask *my* passengers what they wants," replied the ex-warrior quite casually; "an' as to ringin' bells, I leaves that sort o' row to Jim 'ere. You see, mine ain't exac'ly a popular sort o' 'bus, Sir. Nobody fights to get into it, nor seems pertickler anxious to get out again; there ain't much to look forward to, so to speak, at neither end o' *my* route."

Their questioner mopped his face. "Stop a minute!" he implored; "I–I don't understand. Are either of you what they call 'pirates'? I mean, do you work on vehicles not owned by one of the big public-utility companies?"

"We works for the biggest of 'em all, guv'nor," chuckled the ex-sailor. "'Ullo! 'ere we are at Clapham Junction. Good mornin', guv'nor. An' look 'ere—don't you run away with no false notions in your 'ead. You can see our 'buses any day on the London streets, but we ain't no pirates. You see, *I steers a fire-engine, an' my pal 'ere drives a motor prison van!*"

"HOME JAMES."

FOREIGN CHAUFFEURS

"In choosing a chauffeur, too much attention cannot be paid to the factor of nationality, for in no profession do national idiosyncracies assert themselves with greater emphasis."
Extract from a Manual of Motoring

IN motoring matters, the fault of the Dutch
Is their violent method of using the clutch.

Italians and Spaniards will measure their skill
By the number of persons on foot that they kill.

Frenchmen make it an absolute rule
To open the throttle when passing a school.

Russians must stand condemned in a lump
For their habit of drinking the oil in the sump.

The Poles, though good drivers, have one special fault
Of going straight on when requested to halt.

The Swede will cut corners; the Bulgar and Turk
Both put on their brakes with a terrible jerk.

The Austrian's wrong if he thinks he can steer,
And the German is noisy at changing his gear.

The Cretans are liars whose garage account
Is commonly cooked for a tidy amount.

Thus, as each foreign nation we pass in review,
Their faults are apparent, their virtues are few;

And we reach this conclusion: 'tis better by far
To put a true Briton in charge of a car.

Dominion Tyres—Royal Cords, Nobby, Chain & Dominion Treads, creators of new service records—are made at Kitchener, Ontario, Canada, by the Dominion Tire Company.

1920

The Miles You Don't Pay For In NOBBY TREADS

Tyre purchasers usually expect to obtain a certain mileage based on cost—and then fervently hope they may get it.

But everyone's driving experience is marked and marred by bad "tyre bargains"—tyres that give constant trouble—that vary amazingly in performance—that cannot be trusted.

Guesswork and weak optimism need never be associated with Dominion Nobby Treads. They invariably give full mileage value—plus a *good* margin that is not covered by the cost.

The *average* mileage given by a year's output of Dominion Nobbies will equal the *highest* figure of your driving experience with ordinary tyres. There are no "lame ducks" among them.

Added to which they confer real driving safety, freedom from tyre trouble, riding ease which discounts the jolts of "hard going" and distinctive appearance —the benefits of the scientific Nobby Tread.

*Run one Nobby and Check Results
— Beaded Edge and Straight Side.
Nobbies Show the Way to Cheaper Mileage*

United States Rubber Company Ltd.
47-48, Farringdon Street, London, E.C.4.

BIRMINGHAM:
6, Temple Row.

LIVERPOOL:
41-55, Wapping.

GLASGOW:
48-50, Cadogan Street

Dominion Tyres are <u>Good</u> Tyres

MOTORS AND MODES
I—MOTORS
BY OUR FASHION EXPERT

HAD an hour to spare today, B'loved'st, and so just tweaked into the motor show at Olympia. My *dears! The* most charming models one can *possibly* 'magine! Within reach of every pocket is a ducky little Oxley-Cowford—a dream in standard grey, trimmed with deep-toned bugles and electric-blue horns. The brake-shoes are of Veroda, with paste buckle fittings and high wheels.

For those who have *lots* 'n lots of this world's goods there is a very attractive model on the Rolls-Daimler stand, the distinguishing feature of which is the silver bonnet, accordion-pleated at the side, with an adorable little nymph perched coquettishly atop. Six charming *appliqué* cylinders, with inlet valving and exhaust piping, lend an air of distinction, and the whole is d'liciously set off by a *diamanté* fan-belt.

Saw Lady Artemis for a moment. She was in maroon limousine with bold disc-wheel contrasts in aluminium, the tone of which was skilfully repeated on the spare. Her quarterly licence was delicately tinted to match.

Talking of "undies," quite the dinkiest things in crank-cases are to be seen on the Humberhall stand. The main fabric is aluminium and they have a scalloped edge with nut and bolt insertions.

For evening or theatre wear the tendency is towards smaller and more covered-in modes, *coupé* at the waist; while for big functions Isola-Frascatis are again longer this year, and are made to enter from the side instead of wriggling in from underneath.

For bye-bye time there is the Lucendo lighting-set—a poem in silver-plate, liberally volted on each side and with the darlingest little ampères running round the whole.

II—FASHIONS
BY OUR MOTOR EXPERT

Looking in at the next season's dresses this afternoon, I see that Lucille & Cie are showing a nice model of which the chassis work is of black velvet. A universal joint at the waist leads up to the corsage, where appears a small dickey with large carburettor-jet buttons. The cooling system is arranged for by openings in the scuttle-dash near the throat.

Among the Coquin modes I noticed a dear little dance frock with adjustable waist to suit different types of clutch. At the same stand was an evening cloak with hood attached, the interior magnificently upholstered in charmeuse.

Passing the accessories department I picked up for a moment a good toolcase, complete with driving mirror, duster, a tin of Rougeo, valve grinding-powder and screen-wiper.

At the next stand a fashionable narrow skirt caught my eye, curved well round the back axle and specially designed to ensure easy slow running in traffic. List price is five guineas, and it is absolutely ready for a customer to wear away. The same firm are showing some easily accessible bonnets with handy little side-clips for quick removal and inspection.

In the lingerie department I could hardly take my eyes off a most efficient set in which a specially strengthened framework with semi-elliptical springing is used to support a fine range of stocking work in all the most delicate colours, such as mud-brown, pig's-body and gutter-grey. Adjustable brakes are fitted to obviate stocking-slip, while a neat garter acts as a skid-preventive. Near by I noticed a splendid combination in sky-blue which looked to me very fast.

Tea-gowns, I observed, are being made with splashboards this season.

'And do I have to keep on holding this?'

THE BY-ROAD

THE main road swings serenely
　　Across the rustic shire,
Disdainful, calm and queenly,
　　Fit course for racing tyre.
　　　But I prefer the by-road,
　　　The modest humble by-road,
　　　The pot-holed bumpy by-road,
　　With all its dust and mire.

The great cars go careering
　　Along the broad highway.
Past Fords and Cowleys veering,
　　Round charabanc and dray.
　　　But down the peaceful by-road,
　　　The cow-congested by-road,
　　　The bramble-spangled by-road
　　The little children play.

The main road bleakly dashes
　　By village, field and moor,
And straight to London flashes,
　　Where dwell the slum-bound poor.
　　　But down the winding by-road,
　　　The twisty-twirly by-road,
　　　The wriggling, curly by-road
　　You win to Eden's door.

Along the main road streaming
　　The reeking lorries run;
Its surface, tarred and gleaming,
　　Shines oily in the sun.
　　　But give me back the by-road,
　　　The flower-encircled by-road,
　　　The lover-sheltering by-road,
　　Before my journey's done.

I'm weary of the flurry
　　Of cars that bleat and blare—
By day the whirlwind hurry,
　　By dusk the headlights' glare.
　　　I'm off to seek a by-road,
　　　A woodland-shaded by-road,
　　　A silence-haunted by-road—
　　My childhood's dreams are there.

IDYLL.
ANGELA. "Oh, Herbert, don't the petrol fumes smell *much* sweeter in the country?"

FIRST LESSONS IN DRIVING
AIDS TO MEMORY

I TAKE it that in the time of QUEEN VICTORIA the father might instruct the daughter, but never the daughter the father. Those were indeed good old days. I pine for them. I like instructing. Though I am not a schoolmaster by profession I have a large germ of the schoolmaster in my composition—many of us have—and I hate being instructed; and especially I hate being instructed by my daughter; and very especially being instructed by my daughter in the handling of the mechanically-propelled vehicle. Yet that is now my fate. Phyllis has been knowledgeable in such matters for some time; I have hitherto held proudly aloof.

There is, it seems to me, far too little give and take about a car; certainly there is too little give and take about Phyllis. If I do wrong the car takes no cognisance at all of the fact that I am a beginner. And as for Phyllis . . .

"You *will* make the same mistake every time," she complained; "I wonder whether, if I wrote out a few of the main points in words of not more than two syllables, you could learn them by heart."

"There is perhaps something in your suggestion," I answered. "But I remember that when I was young there were in the Latin Grammar certain aids to memory in the form of short poems:-

> 'Common are to either sex / Opifex and artifex . . .'

and

> 'A, ab, absque, coram, de, / Palam, clam, cum, ex and e . . .'

and so on. You see I remember them to this day, and it is nearly thirty years ago. Don't you think you could put your instructions into verse?"

"An excellent idea," said Phyllis. She withdrew to the library, where I found her later, seated with a writing-pad and a wrinkled forehead, and drawing mental nourishment from the sucking of a lead pencil.

"Ah, the rhymes?" I said.

She held up a warning hand.

> "'Vex not thou the poet's mind / With thy shallow wit.'

In three minutes the work will be completed. It is a trilogy. What rhymes with 'water'?"

"Allowable rhyme, 'daughter,'" I suggested.

"Good," she said. More pencil-sucking. Then—"Finis. You will remember your habit of driving with the brakes on? Listen to this:-

> 'A man may be a bigamist, / A forger and a rake,
> And yet not be so base as to / Forget about the brake.'"

"The old fault of over-emphasis, my dear Phyllis—"

"And to this—

> 'Prison for years and years and years / Should be the penalty for such
> As do attempt to change the gears / Prior to putting out the clutch.'"

"I only did that once this morning," I protested.

"And the last of my trilogy—

> 'Petrol and oil and water, / These are the sacred three;
> He who forgets them oughter / Be cast into the sea,
> While his beautiful young daughter / Inherits his property.'"

"Does she?" I cried. "What if my reply to that should be to retire from the unequal contest, engage a chauffeur and reduce your allowance to help to pay for him?"

Phyllis came across the room and placed her hands upon my shoulders, an attitude I have always found disarming.

"You'll never be such a coward as that!" she said. "And as to reducing my allowance . . . Ah! if you only knew all."

"Tell me the worst."

"It isn't the worst. It's the best. When I came in here I began to write a parody of *If*:-

> 'If you can change your gears without a murmur,
> If you can start and stop without a jerk . . .'"

I winced.

"It's all right. *I tore it up.*"

"Because you couldn't find a rhyme to either 'murmur' or 'jerk'?"

"No. Just conscience."

I stooped and imprinted a benedictory kiss upon the top of a ridiculously boyish head.

"My child!" I said in husky tones. "The reduction of allowance is rescinded. In fact, when I can really drive there may be a small increase."

New Motoring Pleasures
await you in the
NEW
BEAN
14~40 h.p.

BEAN CARS LTD
Controlled by Hadfields Ltd
TIPTON Nr. BIRMINGHAM

LONDON SHOWROOMS:
11a, Regent Street
'Phone: GERRARD 7671

AUSTRALIAN DEPOT:
160, Castlereagh Street
SYDNEY

THE
NEW BEAN
14/40 H.P. 5-Seater Tourer
(as illustrated)
£325
DE LUXE SALOON MODEL · · · £395

All essential component parts, including the springs, of Bean Cars
and Commercial Vehicles are made
of Hadfield's famous Sheffield Steel.

YOU'LL BE PROUD TO BE SEEN IN A BEAN

1921

AN OVERLAND HOMECOMING

WHAT a welcome Father will get when he drives home this Christmas in an Overland !

An Overland for a Christmas gift—one that the whole family can enjoy throughout the year. No wonder Mother smiles—and Sis and Billy are radiant.

Father knows, too, that the Overland gives real value for money. Not only in its moderate purchase price, but also in its unusually low upkeep expense. It will save him money in petrol, oil and tyres.

The light weight of the Overland— only 16 cwt.—and three-point suspension Triplex springs give these results on the average:

—28 to 30 miles per gallon of petrol.
—1,000 miles per gallon of oil.
—8,000 to 10,000 miles per set of tyres.

Ask the Overland dealer in your town to show you this car of proved economy. Four models: Touring, Roadster, Sedan and Coupé. Price: £495 for the Touring Car or Roadster, completely equipped. Write for interesting catalogue.

Distributors in all the principal cities of the world.

WILLYS-OVERLAND, LTD.
151-153 Great Portland St., London, W.1

Overland Factory : Willys-Overland-Crossley, Limited, Manchester

RIGHT-HAND STEERING

TO A BICYCLE BELL

ALAS, how many years have flown,
    Since first your silvery note I sounded,
And on a cycle of my own
    First o'er the bumps in boyhood bounded,
And felt, like Icarus, the delight
Of suddenly acquiring flight.

The roads were peaceful then; no noise
    More strident than your ring intruded,
And bells of other little boys
    Who also cycled (as a few did),
And those of elder people who
Sedately pedalled two-and-two.

But the inventive brain of man,
    As restless as the winds that fan it,
Is always making some new plan
    To work commotion on our planet;
Especially it thinks we need
Devices for increasing speed.

So motors came, and all was turned
    From peace to uproar in a twinkle;
The tempest blew, the waves were churned;
    Your modest and melodious tinkle,
Where hooters hoot and Klaxons squall,
Can scarcely now be heard at all.

Lorries and motor-buses dash
    Along the road which was my cycle's,
And charabancs about me crash,
    Sounding a trump as loud as Michael's;
Amid the din it is absurd
To try to make your tinkle heard.

When in the future I retire
    (So runs my fanciful reflection)
And find some land of heart's desire
    Where everything will be perfection,
Motors shall vanish like a dream
And cycles be once more supreme.

Then once again, my bell, you'll serve
    To warn pedestrians encroaching
Upon my path. You'll not unnerve,
    But sweetly hint that I'm approaching,
Nor, like the horn, instil dismay
Into the people in the way.

Gently I'll pedal through the town
    And down the flowering lanes and by-ways,
And nobody shall fly or frown
    At meeting me upon the highways,
And even sergeants of police
Shall smile upon my wheels of peace.

And children, looking close, will tell
    From signs beneath my looks seraphic
That, DANTE-like, I've been in hell—
    The hell of England's post-war traffic;
And they will make it extra nice
For one returned to Paradise.

"Surely that's wrong—he overtook me on the *inside*!"

1927

LINCOLN

It is the nature of man to become dissatisfied with utility alone. Ultimately he endows that utility with grace, beauty, refinement. Man's first home was mere shelter. To-day it is a treasure-house of the arts. The modern car evolves by the same process—from a mere means of transportation to the apotheosis of swift, luxurious mechanical motion exemplified in the Lincoln.

Five-Passenger Saloon

AERO engine design has probably had more influence over the Lincoln than any other car. The principle of "out of step" firing employed in its V-type, 60°, 8-cylinder engine, is a notable example. It results in a complete triumph over periodic vibration, and is mainly responsible for the smoothness of Lincoln acceleration at all speeds. Motorists with wide experience of the de luxe 40 h.p. cars invariably single out this feature of the Lincoln for comment—it is a new perfection in motoring rendered all the more enjoyable by its conjunction with the Lincoln mechanical 6-brake system.

LINCOLN MOTOR COMPANY, DIVISION OF FORD MOTOR CO. (ENGLAND), LTD, TRAFFORD PARK, MANCHESTER

THE PEDESTRIAN SHOW
A COUNTERBLAST TO THE MOTOR EXHIBITION

AS a pedestrian of many years' dodging, I naturally leapt at the opportunity which presented itself the other evening—that of attending the opening ceremony of the Pedestrian Show. Organised by the newly-founded Pedestrians Association, it is the first exhibition of its kind held anywhere in the world, including America.

The President of the Association, who was loudly cheered as he arrived on foot from his home at Little Pootington, opened the exhibition with an appropriate address.

"Mass production of motor-cars," he said, "has sadly depleted the ranks of pedestrians in recent years. But, though we stand with our backs to the wall and may yet be compelled to retreat to the top of it, this last line of defence is impregnable, at all events until a wall-climbing motor is invented."

When the ceremony was over I proceeded on a tour of the Exhibition, now thronged with visitors.

It was encouraging to see the crowds round the stand of the Pedestrians Association, waiting to pay their membership fee and receive a little green or red badge. Green badges are for those whose sympathies with the movement are limited to furthering the safety of pedestrians. For the more extreme or militant party, to which I decided at once to belong, red badges are provided, these signifying that the wearers are not merely determined to make the roads safe for pedestrians but *to make them dangerous for motorists*.

In order to secure badges for my coat, overcoat and mackintosh, I took this opportunity of joining the Association three times over.

Continuing my tour of the hall, I was immediately attracted by an effective display of a new product called "Leapo". At this stand an aged and much-whiskered pedestrian is vividly portrayed in the act of cheating a motorist of his prey by a sensational leap to safety of ten to fifteen feet.

"It's all in the powder," the demonstrator explained to me. "Just enough to cover a half-crown in your morning tea and you're safe even when crossing the top of Whitehall. 'Leapo' means that you can jump twice as far and so live twice as long."

I purchased a large tin of this valuable product.

Another exhibit which caught my eye was the "Resistoflex" armour-plated jacket for pedestrians. The most expensive model is guaranteed to retain its barrel shape even after the wearer has been run over by a steamroller, but the lighter pattern, more moderately priced, is proof against any vehicle up to ten tons in weight.

I invested in a "Resistoflex" jacket, securing also for a small additional payment a belt attachment studded with nails. This, the salesman informed me, was guaranteed to burst any tyre with which it might come in contact.

At the next stand I was introduced to the "Pedestroscope," a neat little mirror which clips on to the shoulder and enables one to anticipate those dastardly stabs in the back which are the cowardly motorist's favourite method of attack. I purchased one of these useful instruments.

"You mustn't miss the 'Wattadin'," loudly observed an assistant at a neighbouring stand; with which he rotated the handle of what appeared to be a miniature loud-speaker and produced an ear-splitting racket not unlike the noise of a heavy lorry bouncing over a succession of pot-holes. It was indeed quite impossible to miss the "Wattadin", and, realising how invaluable the apparatus would be for checking the speed of vehicles approaching round blind corners, I secured one for my own use.

The next exhibit which attracted my attention was a device which I have been on the point of constructing for myself ever since the "white line" system of traffic regulation was introduced on our roads. It consists of a portable "white line" of plain webbing; on a dark evening this can be swiftly laid at some well-chosen point on the road, so that unwary motorists are lured over a steep banking or into some evil-tasting pond. The salesman nodded approvingly at my red badge and threw in an extra yard with my purchase.

In the adjoining Amusement Hall the chief attraction is the "Pedestrians' Paradise," where, on payment of a small admission fee, I

(1) struck three matches on the highly polished sides of a big touring car, leaving ugly trails across the enamel;

(2) inserted a pin into the spare tyre, causing a loud and most satisfying report;

(3) dug my pocket-knife into the all-weather hood, helping to reduce it to ribbons, and

(4) smashed the last remaining fragment of the windscreen.

Feeling much better for this little relaxation I then returned to the Exhibition proper, where the next feature of interest I saw was the exhibit of special lamps for pedestrians.

I was shown a single red lamp attached to a number-plate which fastens to the back of the trousers, and also a set of dazzle lamps with a curious flickering action quite blinding in its effect. I ordered a sample of each.

Closing time was approaching, but I was just able to make a call at the "Decepta" Stand, which specialises in various systems of camouflage for pedestrians. These ingenious outfits give the wearer the appearance of a mile-stone, a cow or a policeman. I selected the third, as most adaptable to my figure.

* * * * * * *

Later—If anybody would care to invest in a large tin of "Leapo", a "Resistoflex" jacket, a "Pedestroscope", a "Wattadin", thirteen yards of portable "white line", a set of lamps, a "Decepta" suit and three little red badges, he had better communicate with me. My wife has just won a motor-car in one of these word competitions.

PEDESTRIAN (*to reckless driver*). "D-don't kill me—I'm on my way—to buy a car—so—I'll soon be on your side!"

"BP" British Pioneer Series

A
Gordon - Bennett Racer

Streamlining was an unknown art in racing car design of 20 years ago, as may be gathered from the accompanying sketch of the Wolseley "Beetle," built for the historic Gordon-Bennett contests.

Nor had taxation, as in these days, any influence on engine size ; for the bore of the "Beetle's" four-cylinder power unit measured no less than 153 millimetres !

It developed 50 b.h.p. at 850 revolutions, which contrasts strikingly with the 5000 or 6000 revolutions per minute common in racing cars of to-day. Its maximum pace was 68 miles an hour.

Two of these cars took part in the 1905 Gordon-Bennett in France, finishing 8th and 11th—the faster of the two driven by the late Hon. C. S. Rolls, averaging 40·4 miles an hour.

Fuel was a less potent factor in securing high speeds in the early days of motor racing than now, when engines are so finely balanced and tuned that only the very best of petrol must be used.

That is why racing men prefer "BP," which contributed materially to the success of the two winners in the last 200 miles races at Brooklands.

For power and speed use "BP"—the British Petrol.

British Petroleum Co. Ltd 22, Fenchurch St, London E.C.3.
Distributing Organization of the
ANGLO - PERSIAN OIL CO. LTD.

"BP"
The British Petrol

NEW HOPE FOR THE PEDESTRIAN

WE pedestrians are so used to considering ourselves as less than the dust upon the road-way under the wheels of the lordly road-hog that it comes as something of a shock to find that there are motoring circles in which our right to set foot upon the road is taken for granted and discussed in so courteous a manner as to suggest a change of heart in our oppressors.

Three simple signals have just been devised by the Motoring Correspondent of a news-paper for foot-passengers to make to motorists. It is sufficiently astounding to find ourselves regarded as persons whose gestures should be worthy of remark, but even more startling to note the tone in which the matter is handled.

The first two simple signals are these:—

(1) "The palm of the hand held outward toward approaching traffic would signify that the pedestrian intends to proceed and would appreciate the slowing-up of traffic."

(2) "Should the pedestrian come to a standstill and make a waving motion with his right hand, overtaking traffic would know that he intended to remain stationary and would allow the vehicles to drive round him."

We, you will have observed, signify that we intend to remain stationary and will *allow* the vehicles to drive round us. This is indeed as things should be. We have regained our proper status and, provided that the traffic sets a due value on gaining our appreciation, the system should work well.

But I cannot help feeling a little bit doubtful about the third and last simple signal, which runs thus:—

(3) "Should he stand still and make circular motions above his head, it will indicate that he is uncertain how to proceed and would appreciate wheeled traffic giving him due consideration until such time as he can make up his mind."

Our right to arrange our thoughts in the middle of the roadway is apparently un-questioned, but we must remember that there are some who never can make up their minds without assistance, and in these circumstances it would be only fair to concede that after a reasonable period, say half an hour, of due consideration the leader of the waiting line of vehicles might slowly advance and very gently assist the waverer in one direction or the other. After all, half an hour would be as long as most of us could make continuous circular motions above our heads without dizziness or exhaustion.

But it is not only in this country that the problem of the uncertain road-crosser has been exercising people's minds. The recommendation of the Paris police in a recent "Safety First" *communiqué* is that "in case of hesitation the pedestrian should fix his eyes steadily on the approaching driver". This sounds much simpler, certainly, than the semaphore method of the third simple signal, but for its efficacy it depends on the possession of a glare of sufficiently high Gorgon-power to arrest the progress of a Paris motor-driver, and which of us can confidently lay claim to this, above all *"en cas d'hésitation"*?

For myself, until I see how this method works with others, I shall continue, in Paris and other foreign places where the roads are broad, to immerse myself in a large English news-paper before starting to cross. Drivers can then see that I am preoccupied and shall probably continue in a straight line, and they can arrange to miss me. At the same time it will be obvi-ous that I am both English and mad and that almost certainly any vituperation in the vernacular would be wasted on me.

THE BACKFIRE

POLLEN HOUSE. CORK STREET. LONDON. W.I.

1926

IN every Renault you have that invaluable asset—
"Reserve of Power." The cruising speed of the
8·3 h.p. Four-seater is 35 m.p.h.; without strain
or effort you accelerate to 45 m.p.h. and over, and
still your engine beats in perfect rhythm. With the
13·9 h.p. model there is smooth acceleration up to
55 m.p.h., again without harshness or apparent effort.
And it is the same with the 17·9 h.p., 26·9 h.p.
and 45 h.p. models, which do 65, 75 and 90 m.p.h.

**The Renault range can be inspected at our Showrooms,
21, PALL MALL, S.W. 1, and trial runs arranged.**

Prices and descriptive literature sent post free on request.

RENAULT LTD., 19, Seagrave Rd., West Brompton, S.W.6

LAMENT OF A CAR

LOCH DUICH swam in sunshine;
  The hills were opal blue;
The car flew up Mam Ratagan
  And groaned to leave the view.
The camshaft twisted round to see,
  The axle's tears were spent,
The pistons whistled angrily
  And—the big end went!

The bonnet saw the Coolins,
  Sgurr nan Gillean capped in cloud,
The radiator boiled with rage,
  The gear-box wept aloud;
The wheels swept round on Sligachan,
  The clutch with grief was rent
To leave such scenes of beauty,
  So—the big end went!

Kyle of Lochalsh was left behind,
  The Coolins sank from sight:
The road to Balmacarra
  Gleamed in the clear sunlight;
The carburettor spat and fumed,
  The engine's spine was bent;
She had turned her back on beauty,
  So—the big end went!

"Excuse me—my dear—but—I have—such—a devastating sense of humour."

THE PEDESTRIAN LUNATIC

I LIKE walking. I like it as an exercise, disregarding its severely utilitarian purpose of conveying the body from one tee to another. It is a difficult confession to make to this generation, but I really like the physical sensations of walking, the rhythmical movements of the legs, the buoyant sway of the body, the deep and regular expansion and contraction of the lungs. And I have a curious belief that walking is good for me, mentally as well as physically.

And so when I have a free day I spend a good deal of it in walking. As much as I can I keep to the open country, the fields, the hills, the woods. But often in the course of my rambles it becomes necessary for me to march along the high road. It is unfortunate, but in Southern England unavoidable.

Tramping over the open country I feel I am one of the wise men of the earth, gathering health with every stride, inspiration, poise, courage to meet and overcome the difficulties of life. But when I get on the high road I cease to be a sage and become a lunatic.

Speaking from my own experience, which seems to be exceptional, I must say that the majority of motorists are kindly, considerate and intensely helpful people. But they are offensive—offensive, not by inclination but from sheer inability to comprehend that any human being can prefer the act of walking to the act of riding in a car and remain sane.

This is the sort of thing that is always happening to me. I believe it must happen to me more often than to anyone else. It would be nice to think (if I could) that this circumstance was due to my personal attractions, but I imagine it is caused by something pathetically appealing, something inherently pitiful about my appearance which I cannot explain but which I would gladly eradicate if it were possible. Anyhow, there it is.

I am trudging happily along an empty road when a two-seater containing a perfectly charming young man and a distractingly charming young lady overtakes me. I shudder, guessing what is to come next. The car slows down and stops just in front of me. The young man turns to me with a pleasant smile.

"Going to Swarding?" he asks.

"Yes," I reply.

"Hop in, then," he says, and leans across to open the door for me.

"Thanks very much," I say warmly, "but I'm walking."

"Yes, I know." He begins to be rather puzzled. "I mean, I see you are. I can save you a good hour."

"I'm sorry," I answer. "I haven't made myself clear. I really *prefer* walking."

The young man looks confused. He is not quite sure that he has heard me correctly. Or he thinks there must be something behind it.

"But I'm passing through Swarding," he says; "and there's heaps of room in the bus. Of course," he adds quickly, "if you *think* it would be rather a squash I can open the dickey-seat. It won't take a jiff."

I shake my head and open my mouth to reply.

"Then my sister will sit in the dickey-seat and you can come in front," urges the young man. "Won't you, Lilian?"

"Like a shot," says Lilian eagerly. "Of course—yes."

"I'm really awfully grateful," I interrupt swiftly; "it's exceedingly kind of you, but I would rather walk. I like walking. In fact I *want* to walk."

It takes much longer than this to convince them, but at last they surrender and drive away. Then they are offensive. They cannot help themselves; I must emphasise that. They look at each other in dazed bewilderment. They shake their heads in a manner which can convey only one meaning. As likely as not the young man taps his forehead with his forefinger, an action which can have only one significance. They have classified me.

Five minutes later in all probability the incident is repeated with slight variations. Lots of them do it. They mean well; I must insist upon that. But it hurts to be judged a lunatic several times in a day.

I suppose I shall have to give up walking. Otherwise, with the ever-growing number of motors on the road, the time will soon come when I shall find I have to confine my pedestrian activities to the grounds of an asylum.

Alternatively I may even have to buy a car.

THE CAR FOR SAFE SPEED

BY APPOINTMENT

Daimler

ALL ROADS ARE STRAIGHT and safe to the Daimler. Its silent sleeve-valve engine endows it with such remarkable powers of acceleration, and so excellent are its qualities of braking, steering and road-holding that, although safety may demand a walking-pace through villages and towns, an average of 40 m.p.h. can be maintained in comfort without involving an unduly high maximum speed. For the Daimler owner, Midland towns are brought within two hours of London's suburbs; while a day's journey of 400 miles is no arduous undertaking.

DOUBLE SIXES:

50 & 30

SIXES:

35/120

25/85

20/70

16/55

THE DAIMLER CO. LTD. COVENTRY

1926 BARKER COACHWORK

40/50 Rolls-Royce " New Phantom " Chassis with Barker Patent Cabriolet de Ville Body, which was sent out to the Argentine for the use of H.R.H. The Prince of Wales during his recent tour

A Barker Body
Acknowledged the World's Best Coachwork

ICH DIEN

BARKER & CO (COACHBUILDERS) LTD

Coachbuilders to H.M. The King & H.R.H. The Prince of Wales

66 & 67 SOUTH AUDLEY STREET · LONDON · W 1

Rolls-Royce Retailers & Body Specialists

CHARACTER OF THE HAPPY MOTORIST

WHO is the happy motorist, who is he
That every man in cars should wish
to be?
It is the generous spirit who, when short
Of clothing and of boots, appears in court
And pays the magistrate with no retort;
Whose long endeavour keeps a rearward
light
Fixed on his number-plate, serene and
bright;
Who, with a natural instinct to discern
Policemen's signals, is yet quick to learn,
Abides by what they say and parks not there
But in some different place, he knows not
where;
Who, doomed to turn about and turn again
With circling cabs, a miserable train,
Shows on his beaming face no kind of strain
But shouts aloud, rejoicing in the dower
Of high taxation on his engine power,
Controls his brakes and gears, for cash
receives
The guerdon of a book with several leaves,
That proves him worthy of the awful task
Of driving as the State may choose to ask,
And one round card, contained in glass, to
prove
The car he drives is privileged to move;
Yet one more book, that registers at need
The car he drives in is his car indeed,
And still one book, by no device obscured,
To show that if he died he died insured;
And thus equipped he makes a sacrifice
Of all that makes earth beautiful and nice;
Bullied by constables and called a toad
He moves in gangs about the slippery road.

'Tis he whom law despises, who depends
On luck for paying visits to his friends,
Who cannot start if it be cold or chill,
Who pays the interminable garage bill;
Whose life is spent amid a constant toil
Of adding grease to grease and oil to oil,
Fears of the failure of electric wire
And the loud burst of the interior tyre;
Who, if he seeks to overtake, will find
The undertaker following fast behind;
Who loudly blows, because compelled, his
horn
Pedestrians or wandering pigs to warn,
Yet if he blows too oft or blows too much
Is called by everyone a such and such;
On whom the rain of broken glass shall fall
Like showers of manna if he hits a wall;
Who, if the unexpected skid arrives,
Rolls in the ditch and faints, and then
revives,
Mixed up with lots of other people's wives.
'Tis, finally, the man who, spite all this,
Detested by the world, retains his bliss,
Transcends, by confidence in feeling great,
His persecuted and impoverished state,
And ceases not to talk, vainglorious,
About the speed and virtues of his bus,
And tells all men the mileage he has done
On how much petrol, each succeeding run;
Looks forward, persevering to the last,
To see his old car by his next surpassed,
And from some secret tank of courage draws
The power to circumvent or dodge the laws.
This is the happy motorist, this is he
That every man in cars should wish to be.

SPEED FIEND (*doing seventy, to friend doing sixty-five*). "What's wrong, George?
Engine trouble?"

THE FUTURE OF MOTORING

I THINK I may claim to view motoring with an impartial eye. When I am in a car I am convinced that pedestrians are a menace to modern progress, and when I am on foot I am broad-minded enough to agree that every motorist ought to be in a cage at the Zoo. Who could be fairer than that?

As I look at this present-day England of ours I perceive three outstanding types of humanity—people who own a car, people who are saving up to buy a car, and people who are trying to sell a car.

There are moments when I ask myself whether our civilisation has produced anything less deserving of the mercy of Heaven than the man who is saving up to buy a car. There are, it is true, occasions when the man who owns a car and the man who is trying to sell a car would look their best on the scaffold, but in their favour let it be said that at most the Recording Angel can only charge them with talking about one particular car, whereas the man who is saving up talks about every car under the sun.

Take such a man for a stroll among the most striking wonders of nature and his eye will lack lustre until a car heaves in sight, when he will brighten up and tell you what make it is and why he has decided not have one like it.

Cars continue to be comparatively expensive because a good engine is still considered to be an important feature. That problem, it seems to me, is rapidly being solved. It should not be long before the quality of the engine will not matter a bean. When the number of cars manufactured has reached such a point that the motorist must crawl in a queue the entire length of the Great North Road and similar thoroughfares, an engine will scarcely be necessary; a sort of punt-pole arrangement will do as well, with perhaps a reaping-hook for cutting away the growing weeds and ivy.

In that tranquil era little children, rousing themselves from slumber, will look out of the family car and maybe catch sight of a man striding across a field. "Oh, Mummy," they will cry, "how fast that man is going!"

"Yes, darlings," Mother will reply with a shudder, "he is what they used to call walking; but don't look or it will make you giddy; and you must promise never to try to go so fast as that. If motoring is good enough for your father and me it should be good enough for you. Now sit tight, because your father thinks we may be moving on another yard or two soon."

It is only too likely, however, that before then someone will have invented a jumping motor-car, a handy little thing in which it will be possible to buzz across country without damaging the scenery too much, and the road traffic jam will be eased off for a time. Hunting will be revived and considerably brightened by such an invention, though it will probably be found necessary to fit the hounds with rear shock-absorbers.

Accepting the grim possibility that motoring will continue to dominate our lives, my suggestion is that we each have a motor-bed and be done with it. With a bed capable of moving under its own power and going practically anywhere there would be no need to get up in the morning and no bother about going to bed at night. And in the event of an accident happening—well, there you are in bed, and under no necessity of cadging one at a hospital.

"Oh, George, what a relief!"
"W-what is?"
"Why, I always thought these wires were electrified."

ABC

In buying a car, as in buying many other things, it is cheaper in the long run to pay a little more in the first place. And infinitely more satisfactory.

A Lincoln has the velvety smoothness, the thoroughbred responsiveness, the continued freedom from repairs that you can *only* obtain in a car of the first rank.

It is built to be the finest car in the world, by men who have the resources to make it so.

Why not take the long view and the short cut? You can buy a Lincoln for considerably less than £2,000.

40 H.P. 8 Cylinders. 6 Brakes.

Chassis Price £980.

You may inspect the Lincoln at 16 Albemarle Street, London, W.1.

Dealers in all important towns and cities.

LINCOLN

LINCOLN MOTOR COMPANY

Division of Ford Motor Co. (England) Ltd., Trafford Park. Manchester.

1927

Tune

Any outstanding achievement expresses a condition of near-perfection best described by "Tune": every record made is a debt to working-harmony, mental, physical or mechanical . . . . . . sometimes all three.

*   *   *

TUNE, in the individual, means FITNESS; the clear eye and the steady hand; the wish and the will to produce and give, on all occasions, one's very best.

Andrews promotes Fitness. It *cleanses internally.* Taken *occasionally,* as need arises, it corrects and disperses the little Ills of Life, safeguarding good Health for all the family through all the Seasons.

*   *   *

Andrews sparkles merrily and is pleasant to the taste. It refreshes and invigorates. In cold weather many prefer the correcting glass of Andrews *"with the chill off."*

Andrews is sold everywhere in the British Isles: 4 oz. Tin 9d., 8 oz. Tin 1/4. For the Tropics, and for Countries necessitating despatch through the Tropical Zones, Andrews is specially prepared to meet Climatic changes and is supplied in bottles.

Andrews Liver Salt

A BONUS FOR CAREFUL PEDESTRIANS

Mr. J. H. DIGGLE, writing to *The Times*, refers to the increased premiums required by insurance companies in view of the growing number of motor accidents caused by excessive speed or careless driving. He thinks it would be only fair to augment the annual abatements allowed for a clean record.

DEAR Mr. Diggle, I agree;
   I call it only fair
To give a man a handsome fee
   Who drives his car with care.

If for a whole continuous year
   His death-sheet he can show
Bearing a record white and clear—
   Or very nearly so,

I feel he ought to have a large
   Abatement on the sum
Which the insurance people charge
   By way of premium.

And still more pay I'd hand to him
   As his undoubted due
Who hasn't maimed a single limb—
   Or only just a few.

To meet the thoughtful driver's case
   This seems a righteous plan,
But I would like it to embrace
   The good pedestrian.

Some bonus surely they should knock
   Off the amount he spent
When he insured against a shock
   Incurred by accident.

If to his name there's no black mark
   To prove he played the jay,
Or pushed a motor off its park
   For getting in his way,

Or killed a charabanc at sight,
   Or laid a lorry flat,
Something—it's only fair and right—
   Should be allowed for that.

VICTIM (*cheerfully*). "It's all right, old man."
MOTORIST. "Well, you needn't be so beastly familiar."

ABDULLA
SUPERB   CIGARETTES

Abdulla's Travelling Companion

LUTRA

Lutra, earth's loveliest Daughter, answers the call of the Sea—
Speeds to the shimmering water, flings back her cloak and stands free ;
Ripples, with tender embraces, lure her away from the shore ;
Cleaving the glittering spaces, she is a Mortal no more.

Out where the grey gulls are screaming, far from sea-gardens and caves,
Lutra floats, lazily dreaming, one with the wind and the waves . . . . .
Sea-nymphs find fabulous treasure, yet she abandons the foam ;
Earth holds an infinite pleasure—naught but Abdulla spells Home.

F. R. HOLMES.

TURKISH   EGYPTIAN   VIRGINIA

PERCIVAL'S NEW CAR

PERCIVAL has bought a new car. He didn't exactly mean to, but he got into a press of people in Knightsbridge going to the Motor-show and found himself in Olympia before he could force his way to the outskirts. Here apparently the impressionable mutt encountered suave and persuasive young men who in rapid succession practically sold him a Crashleigh, a Rattler Six, a Smeltz and a Lightningcrack, besides presenting him with a park-full of miscellaneous paper on the subject of automobiles. They were in the act of further making him the possessor of a new Forrad, complete with two jokes, when a faint suspicion entered their minds. After a heated argument between the various salesmen as to who saw him first it was eventually proved that the Crashleigh stand had prior rights, and under a battery of pitying smiles he was allowed to depart with a Crashleigh and a caution.

Percival was very pleased with his purchase when it arrived. He at once took it round to his pet garage to have a few extra gadgets put on it, for Percival is a dashboard driver, if you know what I mean. He doesn't really mind–like most men–whether the engine is a super-six with overhead valves and emergency exits to all cylinders; nor does he care–like most women–whether the body is nude or woad in colour. All Percival asks for is a good dashboard full of switches and levers and dials, something like the more private portions of a submarine; and week by week he scans the minor advertisement columns of the motoring Press for fresh gadgets as long as he has a spare square inch of dashboard to fill. The result of course is terrifying to any friend who is in the front seat with him, and induces an inferiority complex almost immediately.

By the time Percival had finished with his new Crashleigh the dashboard part of it looked something like a cross between the driver's cabin of the *Flying Scotsman* and an instrument-maker's shop-window. There were switches for every conceivable light, from dashboard light to spot head-light, as well as for the dynamo and the engine; there were gauges to tell you whether you were going up-hill and if so how up, and (needless to say) how much oil there was or which was magnetic north; there was a cover to shroud the carburettor, and a more familiar lever to tickle the carburettor; there was a thing to light your cigarette at, and a thing–though I am not quite sure about this because I was never allowed to try–which gave you a glass of bitter when you pressed the button.

That evening Percival took me out "for a spin, old man". A drive with Percival is always exhausting because when Percival is busy driving it falls to you to read dials and gauges and turn switches. Nothing much, however, happened till the great breakdown. We went out into the country, using every gadget in turn, till we suddenly realised we should be late for dinner if we didn't whizz back at once.

At the top of a hill, however, still some way out of London, a policeman shouted to us.

"What's he want?" asked Percival.

"What speed are we doing?"

"Two-and-a-half," I replied briskly, peering down at the array of instruments, now hardly visible in the dusk, and reading in error the hill-gauge or the beer-dial or something.

"Perhaps I had better pull up and ask what he–" Percival was beginning doubtfully when I had a brainwave.

"After lighting-up time," I explained and grinned broadly. Of all his battery of switches Percival had omitted to use the only one which the law insisted he should.

"Good Lord! Switch on the side-lights quick," cried Percival as he ran over the crest out of sight of the gesticulating Robert.

I reached forward and fumbled wildly. A beam like a search-light leapt from our starboard bow illuminating the road a mile or so into the next county and frightening a meditative road-side cat up to the top of an elm in one-and-half seconds.

"*Side*-lights, not *spot*-light, you fool!" roared Percival as we ran on down the hill. "Or put on the dashboard light if you can't see," he added as, still fumbling in the gloaming, I shrouded the carburettor, set the trip-speedometer back to 0 and nearly started up the cigarette-lighter.

I put on the head-lights, switched the spot off, roved round a bit more and at last got the sidelights on. Then I sank back into my seat. Driving with Percival, as I said, is exhausting.

It was to be even more exhausting, for at the bottom of the hill we had our breakdown. Percival swore and got out, saying we had run out of juice; but we still had, we found, several gallons. So he lifted the bonnet in an efficient manner and peered inside very knowingly.

I sat as still as possible, staring at the winking points of light on the dashboard and hoping to be overlooked. I drew a blank. After two minutes I had to get out and make suggestions for Percival to turn down. Even this did not please; nothing but manual labour on my part would satisfy him. So together for three-quarters of an hour by the beams of Percival's searchlight we dismantled the carburettor, took out and cleaned all four plugs, traced the petrol to its source and tested it to see that it was not water by mistake, inspected the oil and the magneto, and in fact did everything that a skilled mechanic with a *Watson* assistant could possibly have done. Throughout the proceedings the engine (swung repeatedly by me after Percival had used up his self-starter) refused even a single backfire.

At last we pushed the vehicle with the aid of two men at two bob per man to a garage, and while the fellow was dealing with it we used up our last ounce of strength in tottering over to the nearest for a quick.

When we came back the car was going sweetly. The mechanic accepted five bob (I could see I was the only helper who was not being paid for my exertions) and told us he couldn't exactly say what had been the fault, but that he had overhauled everything, and under his charm of manner it had just started up nicely. For this modest confession he got an extra sixpence.

"Now I wonder," began Percival, half-an-hour later for the seventeenth time as we neared home, "what *was* the matter? I noticed that she began to feel funny just after I switched on the side-lights half-way down the hill."

"What?" I cried. "Just after *you* switched on the side-lights?"

"Yes. You were fumbling about so with the switches that I did it myself. Why?"

"Oh, nothing," I said, and was silent.

I am still silent. And now that I have inspected the dashboard again in daylight I am going to keep silent for ever. For, although I thought *I* had turned the side-lights on, it was Percival who had really done it. But certainly at that same instant I had also turned a switch; and there is near the sidelight switch another one, very similar to the touch, which switches the engine on. Or off.

But don't tell Percival, will you, you chaps?

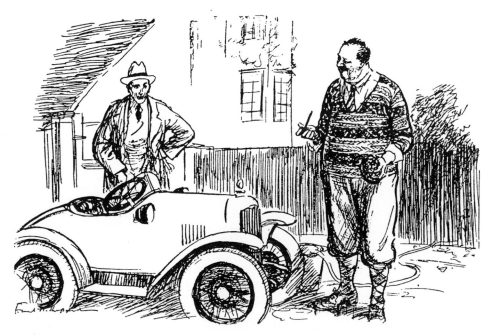

FRIEND (*admiring small car*). "Very nice; but how do you—er—manage to get into it?"
LARGE OWNER. "I don't. I just slip it on."

CHRYSLER CARS HAVE TAKEN THE WORLD BY STORM!

North, South, East or West—no other cars have been so widely and joyfully welcomed as these ! For their effortless silent speed—their thrilling acceleration. For their magical hydraulic brakes—their ease of control. For their vibrationless 6-cylinder engines and 7-bearing crankshafts. Chryslers cover a wide range of prices and sizes and types of car. Chrysler '80.' Chrysler '70.' Chrysler '60.' Go to any Chrysler dealer and see them all for yourself. See how engineering genius such as the world has never known before has brought a new meaning to motoring ! Feel the true fascination of Chrysler—*on the road.* The dealer will gladly let you drive one without committing you to buy !

Catalogues from Chrysler Motors Ltd., Kew Gardens, Surrey

CHRYSLER DISTRIBUTORS THROUGHOUT THE WORLD

INDIA : Automobile Co. Ltd., 5-12 Queen's Road, Bombay ; A. Milton & Co. Ltd., 156 Dharamtala St., Calcutta ; Jones & Co., Madras ; Peary Lal & Sons, Ltd., Kashmir Gate, Delhi ; National Engineering Co., The Mall, Lahore ; Merwanji Edulji & Co., Garden Rd., Karachi ; M. T. Ltd., 41 Rule Pagoda Rd., Rangoon.—STRAITS SETTLE-MENTS : Borneo Motors, Ltd., Singapore.—ARABIA: E. C. Patill, Camp Aden.—CEYLON : Eastern Garage & Colombo Taxicab Co., P.O. Box 206, Colombo.—AUSTRALIA: Larke, Neave & Carter, Ltd., Grenville House, 177-185 William St., Sydney, N.S.W. ;

Collins Motors Proprietary Ltd., Collins St., Melbourne, Victoria ; Ward Motors, Ltd., Box 956 M.G.P.O., Brisbane, Queensland ; O. T. Rodda Motors Ltd., Flinders St., Adelaide, South Australia ; William Attwood, 299-301 Murray St., Perth, West Australia ; Chrysler Motor Co. Pty. Ltd., Hobart and Launceston, Tasmania.— NEW ZEALAND : Todd Motor Co. Ltd., 97 Curtenay Place, Wellington.—SOUTH AFRICA : Carson & Co., 14-16 Riebeek St., Capetown ; Colonial Motors (Natal), Ltd., 183 West St., Durban ; A. Millborrow & Son, 16 and 16a Jones St., Kimberley ; Joseph R. Manning, P.O. Box 195,

Union St., East London ; Clows Motors & Garages, Ltd., 36 Anderson St., Johannesburg ; Messrs. Welsh Brothers, Chrysler House, Russell Rd., Port Elizabeth ; Standard Garage, Ltd., Bloemfontein.—NORTH AFRICA : Hignard Freres, Tunis, Algeria ; E. Brisson & Co., Algiers, Algeria.—WEST AFRICA: Abdo Nasrallah & Cie., 59 Rue Vincens, Dakar, Senegal.—EAST AFRICA: York Garage, Ltd., Nairobi, Kenya Colony.—BELGIAN CONGO: A. J. E. Lock, Compagnie Industrielle Africaine, 1 Standard Bank Chambers, Elizabethville. — RHODESIA : Rhodesia Motors, Ltd., Box 581, Salisbury, Rhodesia.

Chrysler Corporation of Canada, Ltd., Windsor, Ontario

A BUMPER OF BEAUTY AT LAST

CANNOT
RUST

Protection..

A Car without Fenders is so easily damaged. "J.M." Fenders not only improve the appearance of the car, but have the advantages of :

> Great strength ;
> Light weight ;
> Cannot rust ;

and, most important, they are on the mechanically correct principle of rigid bars mounted on shock-absorbing spring buffers.

JMFENDERS
STRONGER THAN STEEL BUT ONE THIRD THE WEIGHT

Ask your Garage to show you a set, or write to the Makers for literature :

"J.M." MOTOR FENDERS LTD.,
SHORT STREET . . . . LONDON, S.E.1.

GEARS AND CLUTCHES

FROM time to time, mostly before the yearly motor-show, rumours are borne on the wind of a new and lovely kind of car that will work without a thing called a clutch and other things called gears. These things, though familiar to the motorist, are mere words to the pedestrian; all he knows is that they are parts of the contraption that comes at him roaring like a lion and gives him a deal of life-saving exercise in long jumps. It is for that kind of person that this article is written. It ought to interest him; it may help him. One has often seen a man, breathless on the pavement of safety, hurling oaths at the back of the car that nearly had him. To curse a great thing like a car is going to do it no harm, but to concentrate the force of your curse instead of distributing it over a wide area, to lay a curse on some one part, such as the clutch or gears, well, it might come off.

I think I may claim to be the man for the job. I have, I believe, a gift of clear and lucid exposition, and I am a motorist of experience, having recently had two (if it wasn't three) lessons. I did this, not with any idea of having a car of my own, but because, when sitting by a driver, I have often wondered what I should do if he were suddenly to have a fit. For one's own skin's sake one would want to be able to stop, even perhaps to drive, the thing. So I mastered the subject.

Briefly, a car consists of two bits, the engine, and—well, the car. Between the two there's a gap. When it's open the engine won't work the car; when it's shut, it will. This gap is closed (or opened, for that matter) by a thing called a clutch. I could tell you all about it, but I shan't. However, there are a couple of facts I may as well put in here. One is that before doing anything you always stamp with your left foot. The other is that driving a car is pretty much like playing an organ. There is a lot for the hands to do—three are wanted—but the broad effects are got by the feet, of which you also want one extra. So much for the clutch. We will now pass to the gears.

These are the devil, and want jolly careful explanation. They come between the clutch, or gap, and the car. At least I think it's like that. They are two sets of wheels, one on each side, engine and car. These wheels are of different sizes and have teeth like pterodactyls or crocodiles, with spaces between them (the teeth). They are done up in a thing called a gear-box, and are fiddled about with by a lever thing; at least yours are, not the engine's. Now these teeth are on the rims, and they move at different speeds because the wheels are of different sizes. You get me?

Very well. The lever is shifted about into varying positions in a thing called a gate; it isn't really a gate, of course; what do you want with a gate in a car? The game is—now, let's be very careful here—the game is, I say—here, dash it, I haven't said that the wheels are moving all the time, but they are—the game is, I repeat, to get the teeth of your wheel, while it's fizzing round, to fit into the spaces between the teeth of the other wheel while *it's* fizzing round. The lever is worked by the hand which isn't steering, and you have to get it into the proper place without looking down. I'm told, too, that if you really make a triumphant bloomer you can actually shear the teeth clean off, in which event the car would get apoplexy. But there's one sweet detail in all this trouble, a thing called neutral. It is the easiest position of all to find; you can't miss it, and when you are there, or rather when your lever is, the blessed and soothing result is that nothing happens; those wheels go round and round, but the car is harmless. You are master.

You may think now that you know all about gears and the use of them. You don't. The detail—the drill, so to speak—of their employment has yet to be unfolded. Before starting on that there are a couple of other things I must tell you about. One is the hand-brake. It is a brake for the hand. As you have only two hands, and as one is busy with the steering-wheel, this hand-brake is put near the gear lever, so that the remaining hand can work both. This would be all right if one could look down; but the gaze has to be glued to the road, and the result too often is that you try to change gear (with no time to spare) with the brake, or, in groping for the brake, get the lever and push your gears into neutral, thus stopping the car.

The other thing is a thing called the accelerator. It accelerates. I don't know how, and it doesn't matter. The mere fact is that the harder you shove on it the faster the car goes. It is worked by one of the right feet, I mean the right-hand feet, so to speak, while the other right-hand foot—but never mind that just now. It is an uppish thing and at tense moments easily forgotten, and, when unexpectedly applied, its effect on an excitable thing like a car is much the same as that of a spur on a jumpy mare on a frosty morning.

And now for the process of changing gear. Upwards it isn't so bad. It goes like this. You start on the lowest and go up one by one. Take up your right foot, shove down your left foot, have a go with the gear lever at the next place, get it in, lift your left foot, shove down your right foot (but go easy) and there you are on number two. Simple, isn't it? The next step up is done in the same way, and so you work to the top.

But working downwards is another pair of shoes. Let me get it right. You take up your right foot, you put down your left foot, you give a dab—no, you don't. Look here, it's like this. The wheel that you want to hoick into the other wheel is going faster—or is it slower? faster, I think—than that other one. Therefore, before you make a dab at it (the other one) it has to be quickened up, or your teeth won't get in. That's it. Now. Left foot down, right foot up, then stick your lever into neutral; left foot down, give the accelerator a moment's gentle reminder, right foot up again, now make a shot at the new position, left foot up, right foot down, and on you go. There. And you do that each time.

I have now in my simple pellucid way told you about the clutch and gears. While I'm warmed up to it, I should like to teach you a lot more—I haven't done with the right foot yet, to say nothing of the mysteries of driving—but for the moment I propose to close down. Perhaps next week (unless I have to play golf)—but we shall see. But there is one thing I must tell you. It is hardly credible, but there actually are persons who deplore the abolition of the things I've described to you because, they say, it will spoil the fun of driving. They call this sort of thing fun.

FIRST MOTOR BANDIT (*to second motor bandit*). "Well, Harold, this is a nice state of affairs. We've been and pinched our own car!"

Picnics have taken on a new meaning since we had our Wolseley! From the door to the heart of the woods in scarcely more minutes than it used to take to reach the railway station! Everything we want —comfortably carried in the Wolseley. What a difference from the old way of trudging with baskets and packages in the dust!

THE flower-decked woods—the sweeping downs—the seaside, are within an hour or two of your door with a Wolseley. And all at a trivial running cost—less than the railway fares for the party would be. Make the most of the long summer-time days—buy your Wolseley 12-32 h.p. *now*. The perfected suspension ensures comfortable riding all the way. The wonderfully responsive engine speeds you along and "eats up" the worst hills. It is so easy to handle that the wife or son can take a turn at the wheel.

12/32 H.P. FOUR-CYLINDER
Touring Car £295   Saloon £315
Coupé £315   Fabric Saloon £330

WOLSELEY

WOLSELEY MOTORS (1927) LTD., ADDERLEY PARK, BIRMINGHAM

THE IDEAL MOTORING COMPANION
With acknowledgements to "The Evening Standard" and Mr. JOHN PRIOLEAU

ONE of the most difficult problems that confronts the owner-driver is that of the motoring companion, and the time has clearly arrived for the licensing of companions as well as drivers. What are the qualifications required in a candidate for this distinction? I will tell you.

In the first place he must pay great attention to his clothes. Loud ties, suits of too assertive a pattern, even brown boots of a certain shade, are apt to disconcert the sensitive driver. If a companion appears wearing a beret, obviously he cannot be allowed to proceed on the journey.

His features too are of the utmost importance. If he has, say, a too prominent nose, a wart on the (right) side of his face or a receding chin he must consider himself disqualified. On the road he must avoid unnecessary speech and, above all, make no comment upon the scenery. Owner-drivers never observe scenery and should not be distracted by being asked to look at it.

Obvious remarks should be strenuously avoided. If at the approach of the car a chicken starts to cross the road and never reaches the other side, such a comment as, "I'm afraid we killed that bird, old chap," annoys the man at the wheel and takes his mind off human pedestrians.

The Ideal Motoring Companion is tactful. If there is a little spill he does not harass the driver by undue curiosity, demanding "How did that happen?" Remarks too about "having a lucky escape," or that it "might have been worse," he uses sparingly. Never in any circumstances does he mention that he "saw the accident coming". That would be presumption on his part, because his brain works slowly; he does not possess the motorist's sixth sense and could not possibly have seen anything of the kind until the accident occurred.

The I.M.C. at all times appears to be enjoying himself immensely, no matter what happens. This is a subtle compliment to the man at the wheel who is good enough to endure his company.

Conversation being discouraged, he has plenty of time to devote to the game known technically as "Spotting the Rattle". By placing his ear to the floor of the car (quite unassumingly, of course), or even leaning over the wind-screen and listening intently, he may be able to locate engine-trouble; but of course he has not the bad manners to report his discovery unless invited to do so. Should a slight repair be necessary he tactfully effaces himself and remains out of sight until the car is ready to start again. Statistics show that 96.3 per cent of owner-drivers prefer to curse unseen. The I.M.C. respects that delicacy of feeling, though he may not always be able to retreat beyond hearing distance.

Attention to the foregoing details will make any touring-companion in a measure ideal, even if he be not a fully-licensed I.M.C., and in his company the owner-driver may enjoy the trip almost as much as if he were alone.

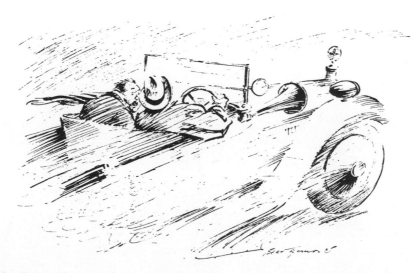

FRESH AIR FIEND. "I say, can't you open the wind-screen and let us have a breath of air?"

1929

You get More out of Life with a

MORRIS

MORRIS MOTORS (1927) LTD., COWLEY, OXFORD.

1928

"All out" with "Ethyl"!

CUT out wasteful low-gear work! Fill up with "Ethyl" and learn the joy of flashing up your pet hill on "top" without the ghost of a knock.

Pratts "Ethyl" Petrol turns carbon (the bugbear of motorists) into additional power, resulting in greater flexibility, economy, and wonderful hill climbing. Sufficient reason why the motoring fraternity are "All out with 'Ethyl'."

Pratts "Ethyl" Petrol is absolutely safe to use. It will not create carbon nor injure spark-plugs, valves or stems. Use it exclusively—dilution reduces its anti-knock qualities. Pratts "Ethyl" Petrol is coloured red simply for purposes of identification. It costs a little more, but you will find that it is more than worth it.

Pratts
Ethyl Petrol

THE JAY WALKER PROTESTS

Fewer people were killed in street accidents last year than the year before.

ONE time whenever I crossed the street
   I felt a delightful thrill,
For I pitted a pair of nimble feet
   And a quite exceptional skill
Against traffic whose speed would not
    disgrace
The scratch machine in a Brooklands race,
And I knew I should be an ambulance-case
If I lost my nerve in that fearful place;
But my Rugger had taught me swerve and
    pace
   And my nerve was excellent still.

But now it is all as clear as a book;
   I am told where I have to cross;
There are signs that tell me which way
    to look,
   And the hand of the traffic boss
Manipulates numerous lights that glow
Red, yellow or green and clearly show
Whether the order is "Stop!" or "Go!"
Or "Wait-for-a-second-and-then-you'll-know,"
And there's only one chance in a million
    or so
   Of becoming a total loss.

The excellent citizen takes a pride
   In obeying the law's behest,
And now as I cross to the other side
   I hope it is all for the best;
But I miss the thrill that the bold must feel
When the hooter shrieks and the brake-
    drums squeal
As he skips from under the passing wheel,
And, although I respond to the bland appeal
Of "Safety First," yet I can't conceal
   That life is losing its zest.

THE DILEMMA

1930

PRICES
Tourer - - - £375
Saloon (all steel) from £385
Club Coupé (Fabric)
with sliding head £399

Triplex Glass Throughout.
Chromium Plating.

BUY BRITISH AND
BE PROUD OF IT.

.....The Isis Six
has stepped easily into
its position of leadership
in the quality car field..

MORRIS

MORRIS MOTORS, LTD., COWLEY, OXFORD.

THE A.A. GIRL

MY little car had begun to splutter and pop and, having no mechanical skill whatever, I was just thinking that the sooner a garage the better, when I saw what looked like an A.A. road-service outfit coming towards me in the gathering dusk. And then, to my astonishment, I saw that the driver of the motor-bike, with its yellow-and-black cabinet side-car, was a girl. My engine petered out as she came abreast of me, and she had passed me by before I hailed her pretty sharply.

"Hi, stop!" I cried.

She pulled up a little way down the road, got off her bicycle and came towards me. I had a good look at her. She was dressed in a kind of A.A. uniform, with a smartly cut brown skirt, gaiters and gauntlets, and a peaked cap set cunningly on her bob. She was an extraordinarily pretty girl and made a perfectly charming picture. How sensible of the A.A., I decided, to start this kind of thing! The feminine patrol; beauty to the rescue. Meanwhile I climbed out of my car.

"Yes?" she said calmly.

"If the patrols do not salute, stop and ask them why," I rejoined.

"Oh, I forgot."

"No police traps, or anything of that sort?" I asked her thoughtfully.

"I didn't see any."

She turned to go.

"Here, steady!" I exclaimed. "For heaven's sake don't leave me. I've broken down."

"What's the matter?"

"I don't know," I replied. "That's for us to find out."

"Us?" rejoined the girl in surprised tones.

"Well, you," I said frankly. "I don't know the first thing about cars; I expect you know a great deal. By the way," I went on, "do tell me, am I right in addressing you as an A.A. guide? If you were a man you'd be a scout, wouldn't you? The opposite number of scout is, I believe, guide."

"I believe it is."

"In that case," I went on, "There's work in the world for a guide to do. An established guide slogan," I explained. "I am sure," I added gracefully, "that it applies to an A.A. guide also."

The girl did not respond to this by flinging open the bonnet or tickling the carburettor.

"It's quite a new idea, isn't it?" I said presently.

"What's a new idea?" she was studying my two-seater abstractedly—"not this car, surely?"

"No, I meant the women's section of your organisation—marvellous, simply marvellous the way women are nowadays absolutely making good. You're quite right," I hastily continued, seeing the look in her eyes, "in supposing that this car is old. It's very old. I got it for a song."

"A part-song?" asked the A.A. girl.

I decided that the A.A. were developing their humorous department.

"Yes," I admitted, and then feeling I must encourage her to grapple with the call of duty I said more sternly, "Would you like an adjustable spanner?"

"I'd like a cigarette," she said, feeling for one.

"Let me—Here you are."

"Thanks so much," she murmured as I lit it for her.

She smoked in silence for a minute or two and I determined to risk a little technical conversation, though my knowledge of cars is most superficial.

"It's a curious thing," I began, "how the contact-breaker's rocker-spindle—"

"The *what*?"

"The contact-breaker's rocker-spindle. Isn't that the correct term? Perhaps you, as a representative of the A.A., can enlighten me?"

"I'm not in the A.A.," she said, "and I don't suppose I know much more about cars than you do. As a matter of fact I'm on my way to a fancy-dress dance at Rattlebury, and I hired the bike from the scout at Little Dithering. The kit is my own idea. Do you like it?" she added more gently.

"Yes, I do," I assured her. "I'm going to that dance too," I went on pleasantly.

"But you were coming away from Rattlebury, weren't you?"

"I must have lost the road," I returned. "Would you be so very kind as to give me something in the nature of a lift?"

"I can give you a lift, I suppose," she admitted. "What about your car?"

"Well, we'll leave it here," I said, "and turn the lights on. May it make somebody happier than it has made me!"

I switched on the lights while the girl got her bicycle running. I then climbed on to the cabinet and sat there cross-legged.

"All right," I shouted cheerfully; "let her go."

"A.A., Sir," she replied, and slipped in her clutch.

The jerk of starting threw me off the cabinet into the road and the motor-bike vanished into the night. Chug, chug, chug . . . And of course the exasperating thing was that I actually was going to that fancy-dress dance at Rattlebury all the time and I really had lost my way. Beneath my all-weather mackinproof, I was dressed, rather appropriately, as a tramp.

THE FRIEND IN NEED

"Hello—a breakdown? Allow me, Madam, I know all about these Titans.

The root of the trouble is often dirty plugs or carburettor choked.

But in this case it may be a stoppage in the water connection.

Or, of course, it may be that your big ends have run out.

Or there is just a chance that your gear-box selector is jammed.

And while we're at it we may as well make sure that the universal joints haven't got torn out.

But in any case it can't be anything serious. I should just wait till an A.A. man comes along."

Here's the Why of the Clincher Y-grip Cord

—the Tyre that makes Winter motoring
as safe and enjoyable as a Summer run

Don't run your car on worn tyres. Be safe this Winter and fit Clinchers—the tyres with the Y-grip.

Clincher is the tyre with the " Y " pattern tread, which prevents skidding, slipping, wheel-spin or any other lost motion in tyres due to faulty road-grip.

On greasy roads—at slippery corners—on awkward hills—in all emergencies of motoring that call for firm road-hold, Clincher Y-grip tyres give a car the sure-footed nimbleness of a cat.

And the tough, resilient centre-pad of thick rubber puts a hard-wearing cushion where the wear is greatest.

Every Clincher carries a guarantee of 7,000 miles minimum. They're good for 20,000. A printed guarantee is packed with every tyre.

The wise replace with Y-grip

NORTH BRITISH
"Clincher" Cords

Not only British. but " NORTH BRITISH "—and Best !

Made in Edinburgh by the North British Rubber Co., Ltd.

GUARANTEED
7000 Miles Minimum
GOOD FOR
20.000

1930

40 H.P. EIGHT-CYLINDER MINERVA LIMOUSINE DE VILLE—£2050

"*The* WONDER CAR *of the* YEAR!"

(*Vide* Capt. de Normansville, DAILY CHRONICLE, 26.9.1930.)

Here is, indisputably, the most perfect combination of Luxury, Power and Safety ever known in car construction. A new stabilising device makes skidding impossible .. eliminates all swaying or tilting of the Coachwork on corners and uneven surfaces . . . and ensures smooth, safe, and silent travel at the highest speeds of which it is so easily capable. In *every way* worthy of its reputation as "The Wonder Car of the Year."

OTHER MODELS: 40 h.p. 8 Cylinder Minerva Limousine . . £1875. 32-34 h.p. Limousine or Landaulette . . £1400. 6 Litre "Speed Six" Chassis . . £1100

Head Office & Showroom: CHENIES STREET, LONDON, W.C.1

PEDESTRIAN-COURSING

Being an extract from the correspondence columns of "The Spectator," February, 1948.

To the Editor of "The Spectator"

SIR,—It seems to me that the whole question of pedestrian-coursing has become obscured by a very deplorable sentimentality. Surely the fine qualities fostered by this sport—qualities, Sir, of endurance, nerve and initiative, which have made the British Empire what it is to-day—are of more value to the nation than the lives of a few score pedestrians; and after all, as GLADSTONE so wisely remarked in 1875, "we have no evidence that they do not themselves enjoy the sport"

I am, etc.,   BOANERGES BULLOCK
Pall Mall   (Lt.-Col.)

To the Editor of "The Spectator"

SIR,—And Beauty? Has she no longer any voice in the councils of the nation? Is Pity to be thrown to the economists? The pedestrian, Sir, is one of the most charming little animals indigenous to this country, and we discuss its extermination as calmly as we would that of a politician.

Not long ago I happened to be motoring through the Lake District and came upon a family of these timid creatures feeding under an oak-tree. At my approach they stopped eating and, impelled by the mysterious instinct of their race, scurried across the road in front of me. To the disgust of my coursing friends in the back *I slowed down*; and I shall never forget as long as I live the look of startled and pathetic gratitude they flung me as they reached the other hedge.

I am, etc.,   ALOYSIUS GUMM
Golders Green

To the Editor of "The Spectator"

SIR,—Your correspondent R.R. has, I think, hit the nail on the head when he refers to the importance of this sport to the motor industry; but he has not hit it hard enough.

He mentions the enormous number of workmen employed by the various British motor factories, but he might have added that this sport has done more than anything else to improve the standard of cars and to form a great reserve of vehicles on which the Government can call at need. In the event of another Four Years' War—which Heaven forbid—we should be able to call up at least a million first-class cars from private garages only. Is this nothing?

I am, etc.,   SI PACEM QUÆRIS
Westminster

To the Editor of "The Spectator"

SIR,—It may interest your readers to know that as early as 1927 (more than twenty years ago!) a movement was already on foot to check this cruel sport. In quite a slight case of running-down a London magistrate is reported as saying:

> "The pedestrian has as much right to the road as anyone else; and if I had my way any motorist responsible for more than four fatal accidents in one month *should have his licence endorsed.*"

The italics are mine.

I am, etc.,   JUSTICE
Outer Temple

To the Editor of "The Spectator"

SIR,—Pedestrian-coursing is one of the few open-air amusements which do not show signs of decay, and no unbiassed critic would deny that it has its roots deep in the sporting instincts of the British people. But that there are abuses is unfortunately only too evident, and it is time that the rulings of the P.C.C. were thoroughly overhauled. If the pedestrian could reason I think his line of thought would be something like this:—

(1) There should be certain limits to any run, after which I should be considered to have got away; for instance, no pedestrian started in Piccadilly Circus ought to be pursued further than Parliament Square.

(2) The island refuges should be inviolable, and "shunting-off" by mounting the kerb ruled out.

(3) No driver should be permitted to cut in on another man's pedestrian from a side-turning, and any heading-off by casual motor-cyclists should be discouraged.

(4) All traffic-blocks should count as natural hazards, of which the pedestrian is allowed to take advantage by getting lost or using police protection.

I am, etc.,

THE LITTLE FLAT FOOT.
Pimlico

We agree in the main, but at the same time one must remember that nothing kills a game so quickly as a surfeit of conventions; look at what happened to Bridge.—ED., *The Spectator.*

CAR TOPICS

I HAD a little *———**—* Nine;
 I kept it *———**—* years;
It had a *———**—* body-line,
  And *———**—* *———**—* gears.

The chassis had a *———**—* spring;
  It had a *———**—* hood;
And why I bought the *———**—* thing
  I never understood.

The sparking-plugs were *———**—**———*;
  The brakes were *———**—**———*;
The steering-gear was *———**—**———*
  *—**———**—* *———**—* *———*;

And when a *———**—* *———**—* *———*
  Ran into it, the cad!
I own that I was *———**—* *———*
  *—**———**—* *———**—* glad.

AUNT (*frigidly*): "Tell me, Hector, Is this an accident, or
merely another thing that the car can do?'

1929

February-proof!

The usual severity of February's weather provides a *real* test for your car's finish. The man whose car is 'Belco' finished can confidently leave it out-of-doors in *any* weather. 'Belco' is impervious to frost, rain or mud. Neither time nor exposure can diminish its flashing beauty—and a few rubs with a cloth keeps it like new. That's why the experienced motorist always insists on

Specify 'Belco' on your new car

NOBEL CHEMICAL
FINISHES LTD.
(Associated with Imperial
Chemical Industries Ltd.)
SLOUGH, BUCKS.

'Belco'
THE *BETTER* CAR FINISH

C.F.H.

THE FRONT-SEAT COMPLEX

IT is an extraordinary thing but the best and most expensive of cars never seems to be quite right when I am in her. Her owner is invariably peeved about something, though to listen to him at dinner the night before you would suppose she was the last word in virtuous efficiency.

Nothing has a more chastening effect upon me than to sit in front with an owner-driver. However light-hearted I may be at the start the owner-driver will get me down in time. It probably happens that so far as I am concerned everything is lovely—the day, the air, the scenery and the purring ease and rhythm of our progress. Experience, however, has taught me that behind this blissfulness there lurks an evil of which I am contemptibly ignorant. The darkly-brooding man beside me knows what it is, and since his mute suffering has already tinged with melancholy my rapturous exhilaration I may as well get the credit for being less of a boob than I feel.

So I put on a critical frown and lean forward attentively with lips slightly pursed.

"Yes," he says gloomily, yet with some relief at being forced to speak about it, "she's knocking badly."

If she isn't knocking badly then she isn't pulling well, or she isn't as sweet as she might be. It seems I jolly well ought to have been in her the other day when her equal was not to be found in heaven or upon earth.

It always is the other day. Can it be that the fault is mine and that I have a bad effect on my friends' cars? I only know that whenever I get in one she ceases to be sweet or she knocks or doesn't pull. I never notice it myself. She seems to my simple comprehension to be giving of her best, judging by the gleam in the eyes of traffic policemen and the way pedestrians skip like joyous lambs about her bonnet.

It shames me that I should be enjoying myself so thoughtlessly, and I do my best to feel as my friend feels about it. I listen for noises which are not there, and nod my head with appreciative sympathy when he moans, "Hear that?" until at last the front-seat complex has me in its grip and I really do believe the whole car is groaning and travailing in pain. I wonder how long it will be before the engine drops out or the rear axle breaks, and what they will put on my tombstone.

I am now hearing almost as many noises as my friend hears. The din is frightful, and I marvel that the car holds together at all. In the back seats the women are chattering gaily as if they were determined to show no sign of the terror which possesses them.

"This is glorious," cries one, breaking off from the subject under discussion.

"Perfect," agrees the other, the owner-driver's wife. "The car's running extra well to-day."

Good Heavens! are they deaf?

ABSENT-MINDED YOUNG POLICEMAN (*newly transferred to the mobile squad*).
"Warm enough, darling?"

1930

MORRIS OXFORD

SIX CYLINDER · FABRIC SALOON · PRICE £285 EX WORKS

NEW COLLEGE   MORRIS MOTORS LTD. COWLEY, OXFORD.

ROMANCE AND THE MOTOR-CAR

WAS it not there where the long hill winds,
  Woods to the left and the plain below,
And the world a dream that the dreamer finds
  (Ah, how many years ago)–
Was it not here when the light lay clear
  Over the grasslands, over the loam,
That we suddenly punctured a tyre, my dear,
  One hundred miles from home?

Memories still come thronging back
  Of the high-blown clouds in the front of Spring,
Of fooling about with the agéd jack
  Till we finally smashed the thing;
And the birds were loud in that woody place,
  The shining valley was filled with peace,
And you had mud on your hands and face
  And I was all covered with grease.

And I seldom look at a grey stone town,
  And I seldom gaze at a field of stubble,
But I think of a place where the car broke down
  On account of magneto trouble;
And the buttressed bridge where the stream runs strong,
  The swift stream running from shallow to pools–
It was there that we sighed so long, so long
  For an A.A. man with tools.

Faint and few were the flowers that showed–
  Ah, do you remember the lanes we thrid
Trying to get to a first-class road
  On the day we had that skid–
The little lanes in the heart of the shires
  That moved our minds with a delicate doubt
Because of the keen flints under the tyres
  And the hobnails lying about?

And was it not there, by the ruined farm,
  By the ruined farm where the gate hangs loose,
That we felt the shade of a sick alarm,
  Being almost out of juice?
Was it not here, where the light lay clear
  On the broken byres and the desolation,
That suddenly round the bend, my dear,
  We discovered a petrol-station?

1930

It was the directors' decree—

the new Humbers *must* be the world's finest car value in
the quality class. The word went round. Efficiency was
the order of the day. Rationalisation. Perfect organisation.
And in the 1931 Humbers this wonderful ideal is realised
to the full. You are invited to send for the new art
catalogue which describes and illustrates these fine cars.

"16/50" Saloon   "Snipe" Saloon   "Pullman" 7-Seater Saloon
£425.   £485.   £695.

Triplex Glass on all models.

HUMBER

OVERSEAS REPRESENTATIVES:—
Australia and New Zealand—Mr. C. E. Blayney, Rootes Ltd., Herald Buildings,
    Pitt Street, Sydney.
India and Ceylon—Mr. H. H. Lilley; P.O. Box 803, Bombay, India.
South Africa—Mr. H. C. Leon, Rootes Ltd., 40/40a, North British Buildings,
    C/R Commissioner and Simmonds Street, Johannesburg.
Burma, Malay and Far East—Mr. A. F. Sanderson, P.O. Box 525, Singapore.
Europe—Mr. R. Escudier, Devonshire House, Piccadilly, London, W.2.
South America—Mr. R. W. H. Cook, Banco Anglo-Sud-Americano, Buenos Aires.

HUMBER LTD., COVENTRY.

London Showrooms and World Exporters :—
Rootes Ltd., Devonshire House, Piccadilly, W.1.

AGAIN—SUCH CARS AS EVEN HUMBER NEVER BUILT BEFORE.

SHAKESPEARE AS MOTORIST

AN American professor—mostly American, I fancy—has recently had an urge to tell the world that the guy WILLIAM B. SHAKESPEARE is out-of-date—is, in fact, the back leg of a lame tortoise.

All Americans, however, do not think this. Mr Attaboy D. Hoosh, that well-known lover of the high spots of Parnassus (Gre.), has, on the contrary, just produced a booklet proving conclusively that SHAKESPEARE knew all about motors, for instance, centuries B.H.F. (Before HENRY FORD).

By his vurry kind permission I am enabled to quote from this work, which will, as he says, "can the boneheaded cackle about old man SHAKESPEARE being a back number". It is arranged in the form of quotations, and I will let it spiel for itself:—

Engines (Noisy)—

"Thou . . . in complete steel
Revisit'st thus the glimpses of the moon,
Making night hideous."   — *Hamlet, I. 4.*

Engines (Difficulty in Starting)—

"Which, much enforcéd, shows a hasty spark,
And straight is cold again."
            —*Julius Cæsar, IV. 3.*

Engines (Over-oiling)—

"The rankest compound of villainous smell that ever offended nostril."
            —*The Merry Wives of Windsor, III. 5.*

Insurance Policy (Flaw in)—

"Never did base and rotten policy
Cover her working with more deadly wound."   —*Henry IV., I. 2.*

Mass Production—

"The baby figure of the giant mass."
            —*Troilus and Cressida. I. 3.*

Mechanics—

"Another lean unwashed artificer."
            —*King John, IV. 2.*

Motoring Offences—

"I'll put a girdle round about the earth
In forty minutes."
            —*Midsummer Night's Dream, II. 2.*

"All his faults observed,
Set in a note-book, learned, and conned by rote."   —*Julius Cæsar, IV. 3.*

Petrol (Advertisements for)—

"A rarer spirit never
Did steer humanity."
            —*Antony and Cleopatra, V. 1.*

"The spirit of the time shall teach me speed."   —*King John, IV. 2.*

Petrol (Water in)—

"These foolish drops do something drown my manly spirit."
            —*Merchant of Venice, II. 3.*

Traffic (Block in).

"Why, one that rode to his execution
Could never go so slow."
            —*Cymbeline, III. 2.*

Traffic (Police Control)—

"Look with what courteous action
It waves you on."   —*Hamlet, I. 4.*

Traffic (Lights Control)—

[GO]   "The ground is tawny
Yes, with a green eye in't"
            —*The Tempest, II. 1.*

[STOP] "Making the green one red."
            —*Macbeth, II. 2.*

Tyre Trouble—

"Let me not burst."   —*Macbeth, I. 4.*

"Here will be an old abusing of God's patience and the King's English."
            —*The Merry Wives of Windsor, I. 4.*

"My high-blown pride
At length broke under me . . .
Vain pump* and glory of the world, I hate ye."   —*Henry VIII., III. 2.*

These extracts should of themselves be enough to convince anyone, thinks Mr Attaboy D. Hoosh, that SHAKESPEARE was a motorist; but his attitude to pedestrians puts the matter entirely beyond doubt:—

"You are not worth the dust which the rude wind
Blows in your face."   —*King Lear, IV. 2.*

So thorough-going was he and so wonderfully provident was his mind that he could even supply an excuse for joy-riding three hundred years before it was actually needed:—

"He that is robbed, not wanting what is stolen,
Let him not know it, and he's not robbed at all."   —*Othello, III.3.*

In conclusion, Mr Hoosh, who is a great admirer of internal textual evidence, draws our attention to *The Merry Wives of Windsor*. In this play, it will be remembered, a certain *Ford* did undoubtedly request *Sir John Falstaff* to take half a bag of money, or all of it, for "easing him of the carriage"; and when, later, *Ford* asked him how he had sped, the reply was, "Very ill-favouredly, Master Brook." This point, says Mr. Hoosh, will surely carry conviction to any guy, even a Baconian. I hope it will.

*Some versions prefer "pomp," an obvious archaism.

SPRINGTIME ON THE ROAD

THE sun shone; Spring's lively zest stirred in
  my marrow;
    Green flashed the hedgerows and the grass;
Then I came up behind you where the road was
    narrow
    And you would not let me pass.

I tooted my horn, gently at first and mildly,
    As who should say, "Thank you, friend,"
    But you clung to the road's crown and swept,
      swerving wildly,
    On the wrong side round the bend.

You waved me on in a rude derisive manner,
    While holding me still in check,
Till I hurled indignant oaths, and almost a spanner,
    At the back of your fat neck.

The road widened at last; at this hopeful juncture,
    As I muttered, "Ah-ha, my lad!"
A voice from the back said, "George, have we got a
    puncture?"
    And it turned out that we had.

Away you sailed, leaving me flat as a flounder,
    With a last contemptuous honk,
And I fear you heard me not when I yelled, "You
    bounder,
    May your big-end conk!"

"Well, anyway, the mascot's all right, Ted. I told you it was lucky."

THE BOAT RACE

Everyone loves this typically English event in which pluck and preparation alone give that margin of difference that wins. It *is* like the difference of Shell petrol, which is balanced and re-balanced from ingredients tested and re-tested until it attains a perfection that wins in every test where sheer efficiency counts

THE DIFFERENCE—Shell petrol is blended from sources some of which are exclusive. The essentials—anti-knocking, chemical cleanliness, easy starting and rapid acceleration—are so balanced in Shell that none is absent and none developed at the expense of another

SHELL
petrol is *different*

1931

The MORRIS-COWLEY
SALOON
£185

Triplex Glass &
Chromium Finish Standard

WITH FOLDING HEAD £190 (*PRICES EX WORKS*)

BUY BRITISH AND BE PROUD OF IT

THE CAR THAT WAS

FOR the last week every person I have met has said at one time or another, "And have you been to the Motor Show yet?" I have invariably answered "No!" At the resultant look of mingled pity and incredulity I have added: "And I am not going either". After which, of course, they have looked over and through me and I have passed out of their lives. Poor simp! He doesn't understand.

But it was true. I did not go. Olympia was full of the latest types of motor, the most modern engines and chassis and body-works and what-not, and I didn't give a cuss. *My* heart was in the past. For motoring nowadays is not what it was. Too uneventful in the actual driving, too lacking in incident on the journey. You can start out to go a hundred-mile trip in the morning in the zest-destroying certainty of turning up in time for lunch, with the dull record of your journey writ only on the speedometer, instead of all over the car. You can calculate the cost of running for the next six months with depressing accuracy. You can't have a nice rattling friendly vehicle without being run in and told to abate it. You can't leave the old juggernaut anywhere for a moment except in specified places, and then only for a moment. You can't—oh, well, maybe I'm biased; for once *I* had a car. . . .

It was my first car, and it was a wonderful bit of work. It had the engine somewhere at the back, I never was quite certain where, and the handle stuck out at the side (always the *other* side), and the whole affair boiled quicker than an egg-cup of water in the heart of a blast-furnace. It needed water therefore about five times as often as it needed petrol, and I used to go out with wicked-looking kegs strapped all along the running-boards, which gave me the air of a bootlegger crossing the border.

Despite this I became a well-known menace to all the Service Stations (Water Free) within a fifty-mile (or four-gallons) radius round London. One of them, I was afterwards told, once filled up my radiator with petrol in a determined attempt to get rid of me, but if this is true I never noticed it. Maybe it just wasn't good petrol.

There was an electric-lighting set on that car, but from the moment that the man who was selling me the thing said, "Lights all right, you see," and switched them off, they never lit again. But it didn't matter much. There was generally a bright red glow from the exhaust-pipe at the rear, sufficient to illumine my registration-plate, and an intermittent flashing from something misguided and electrical in the front, so I think I could have travelled by night if I had wanted to. And there was a pillar of steam by day.

It was heavy on tyres, if I remember rightly. At least it used four in the first week after purchase—an average of one every nine-and-a-half miles. Subsequently I noted an improvement.

On the other hand it was light on oil. It hardly *consumed* any oil. I speak advisedly. But as an oil-filter it was perfect. It could filter oil from the engine to the road surface (or to a bucket underneath when stationary) at the rate of a quart every fifty minutes. All impurities, waste matter and grit were guaranteed to be retained, and only the pure oil passed through.

The braking system was unique. In the first place—either by the passage of years or else some peculiar mechanical device—when I pressed the footbrake, it and the accelerator and clutch all went down together. This made my slowing-up in an emergency a very impressive performance and generally cleared everything off the road so quickly that the brake need never have been used. Perhaps that was the idea.

The hand-brake was situated somewhere on the outside. Standing in the road I could always locate it quite plainly, but when once I was inside I was never quite sure of its exact position. In bad weather I had to unbutton and let down the hood to get at it. It was only an emergency brake, but by the time I was ready to use it the emergency had always passed on.

I often wonder what eventually happened to that car of mine. Late one memorable evening, returning to Town from Brighton, I was half-way up the steep Reigate Hill when the top of the radiator suddenly blew off as a protest. There was of course a loud roar, clouds of steam and a sudden stoppage, but at first I didn't know anything out of the ordinary had happened. Then I realised that the steam was much thicker than usual and smelt quite different, so I got out. By this move I also detected a burst in one back tyre and an abnormally large flow of oil from a new place underneath. Night also was falling and the lights, as I have said, had never worked and didn't work then.

I confess I became discouraged at this slight mishap, but you must know I had then been three-and-a-half days on the road from Brighton, and had an important engagement in Town on Thursday.

So I lost my temper. I walked round the thing, cursing it; I kicked it on the other back tyre (which promptly burst in sympathy), and then I took a strong line. Washing my hands of the whole darn thing, I walked back down the hill to the station.

You will probably not believe me (though it's perfectly true) but I have never seen that car since.

About two months afterwards I had to refund five shillings to the Automobile Association, a reward paid on my behalf to a man who had found my "A.A." badge. It had been in my day on the top of the radiator, but the finder reported he had discovered it in a field three hundred yards from any road.

When at weddings or in my cups or otherwise sentimental I often wonder what really happened to My First Car. Those were the days, begad, when a gentleman felt he *had* a car when he went out, and when he *could* leave a car anywhere he liked. Ah well! *Forsan et hæc olim meminisse juvabit Automobilia.** But doubtless you know your HOMER.

*But perhaps one day it will help to remember even these motorcars

THE EGOIST
"Here, you—come and look what you've done to my mudguard!"

These Liverpool directors have chosen the Buick:

T. H. COOKSON, ESQ.,
Director, *E. H. Perrin & Co. Ltd.*

H. S. DAVIDSON, ESQ.,
Managing Director, *R. Davidson & Co. Ltd.*

H. J. GORDON, ESQ.,
Managing Director, *Thos. Rigby & Co.*

G. H. POTTER, ESQ.,
Director, *W. H. Potter & Sons Ltd.*

" . . Porlock Old Hill with four up. . "

" My Buick 6-cylinder Saloon is in use every day and has now completed 40,000 miles with a total expenditure for replacements of £1 11s. 8d., which I consider excellent. She is very fast and holds the road at speed. Last July I left Glasgow at 6.45 a.m. for London. I stopped for three quarters of an hour to fill up and have something to eat, and arrived in London at 9.40 p.m. Respecting hill climbing I have taken Porlock Old Hill with 4 up and 1 cwt. of luggage and not been below middle gear. I have had 29 years' driving and during that time I have owned most makes but this is the best car I have owned and driven."

F. SEYMOUR SMITH
*6, Burgess Road, Bassett
Southampton*

This year is the Silver Anniversary of the Buick motor car. Its twenty-five years of leadership are easily understood if you examine the 1929 models.

But you cannot really appreciate the Buick without giving it a severe trial. Any dealer will be glad to give you a demonstration run. To those who are interested in the doings of General Motors a cordial invitation is extended to view the factory at Hendon. Write for an interesting booklet : " Down Hendon Way."

Write also for a catalogue showing the complete range—£425 to £695. General Motors Limited, The Hyde, Hendon, London, N.W. 9.

The best salesmen for the Buick are the great army of enthusiastic Buick owners Read this typical letter from one of them and learn what they mean when they say " a top-gear car." Then ask any dealer for a demonstration run

1931

ICH DIEN

BY APPOINTMENT
TO H.R.H. THE PRINCE OF WALES

MO 1931

THE QUALITY OF

MORRIS

IS THE REASON FOR ITS FAME

Dorland

MORRIS MOTORS, LTD., COWLEY, OXFORD
CHROMIUM FINISH   TRIPLEX GLASS THROUGHOUT

BUY BRITISH AND BE PROUD OF IT

A COMMON INFORMER

THE THATCHED HOUSE,
SWEETCROFT LANE
March 1930

To the Superintendent of Police

SIR,—One of the pleasures of my semi-rural existence is the walk to the station in the morning. For some time now, however, that pleasure has been marred by a young female motorist who flashes down the lane at fifty miles an hour and temporarily devastates the entire region.

Far be it from me to suggest that our dashing young females ought to be unduly restrained (for what is man in this age of rampant feminism?); but it occurs to me that, if one of your constables happened to be on early duty in the lane, he might put in a bit of useful work. But let him wear an identification disc in case his agility is not equal to his good intentions.

I am,   Yours truly,   TOBIAS MIDDLEMISS

I sealed and stamped the letter with some satisfaction; it had just the right snap. Then I glanced at my watch. Heavens! it was 9.20. In the throes of composition I had forgotten the time and I had an important appointment in town. I seized my hat and dashed out. It was hopeless, of course, but I kept it up for forty yards, then slowed down, gasping. Confound the girl! She had now crowned her other misdeeds by making me lose my train on the worst possible morning. If only—A hum smote my ears, a roar, a scrunch of brakes and finally a silvery voice inquiring in friendly tones if I needed a lift.

It was she. For a brief moment I felt inclined to unseal my letter and read it to her on the spot, but this would clearly involve refusal of the proffered help. Besides, on a nearer view she was much prettier than I had imagined.

"Thanks," I said stiffly, "it is of the utmost importance that I catch the 9.30."

She whistled. "You've cut it rather fine, you know. Jump in."

We should have done it comfortably if it hadn't been, first, for an idiotic flock of fowls and, second, for a man with a barrow who in spite of repeated hootings persisted in maintaining the middle of the road. As it was, the last half-mile was a rather hair-raising affair and I breathed a sigh of relief as we flashed up to the station just as the train was snorting in.

As I dropped into my corner-seat I could not help smiling at the irony of the situation. If only she had known the contents of the letter I carried, how she would have stared. Run me to the nearest pond probably and tipped me in. The sooner that letter was torn up the better. I felt in my pockets. What on earth had happened to it? A feeling almost of horror came over me. In my scramble I must have dropped it in the road—or in the car.

Gracious! suppose the girl herself—But no, it was sealed and stamped, and the worst anyone could do was to post it. Confoundedly annoying, though. Almost like an act of treachery. I should have to warn her now. Without committing myself, of course. Just tell her I had heard the police were on the war-path. It was the least I could do.

*   *   *   *   *   *   *

I had just finished dinner when a constable was announced. He came in, a ruddy-faced man with a merry eye. I greeted him with tactful affability.

"This is very kind of you, Officer," I said.

"Instructions, Sir," he answered briskly. "The Super said as I was passing this way on me bicycle I might as well look in and acknowledge your letter."

"Very thoughtful of the Superintendent."

"One of the best letters he ever read, the Super said it was, Sir."

I smiled; the police had a keen sense of humour, it seemed.

"May I ask what steps you propose to take?" I asked.

"Well, it's a funny thing, Sir, but we took action before ever we got the letter. Me and a plain-clothes man timed her this mornin'."

For a moment I did not quite grasp the dreadful significance of this, then a cold sensation started at the base of my neck and crept slowly down the spine. "This—this morning?" I faltered.

"Yes, Sir, from Tinkler's farm to the village. And she wasn't half moppin' along."

"Good gad—I mean—er-good."

Heavens! Why, they must have seen me mopping along with her. Me, the writer of the letter, accusing her of mopping along. An odd sort of limpness came over me. Surely the fellow must recognise me? Yet apparently he didn't. I strove to pull myself together.

"Does—does the lady know about this?" I murmured.

"Oh yes, Sir. I came up with her at the railway station and told her she'd be reported for a summons."

"W-what did she say?"

She said, "Oh, hell!"

"Quite. I mean was that all?"

"That was all, Sir."

I took heart. There was evidently nothing to identify me as the passenger, and my obvious course was to reimburse the girl the amount of her fine and lie doggo.

"I only wish I could get the gent who was with her for aiding and abetting," continued Robert with some feeling.

"Oh, there was a gent with her, was there?" I asked, growing still more confident.

"There was, Sir. Eggin' her on too. I reckon he was worser than what she was."

I coughed. "Some of these—ah—middle-aged gents are worser—worse than the young ones," I ventured.

"Not half they aren't," he chuckled.

"But you can't get him, you say?"

"Well, Sir, it's her car, you see, and she was driving it, so we can't hardly—"

"Of course not," I put in hastily. "Well, I must thank you for your courtesy. By the way, when did you get my letter?"

He rose and took his helmet from the table before replying. "When the young lady give it to me at the railway station, Sir," he said, and it seemed to me there was suddenly a wicked twinkle in his eyes. "You see, she found it on the seat just after the gent got out, and she said, as it was addressed to the police, I might as well have it. Oh, and I was to say," he added with a ghastly chuckle, "that the Super proposes to read the letter in court. Good day, Sir."

FAIR LEARNER. "Oh, Ted—quick! Here comes the hedge!"

YOU find a new thrill in motoring—in an England Body. A sensation so new that you notice it the moment you take your seat—a sense of peace and comfort, of tranquillity, and swift—sweeping—flight. For with the roominess and beauty of England Bodywork goes a lightness and efficiency in construction that lends wings to the fastest car. An illustrated booklet containing a full description of England Bodywork, and a list of the cars on which it is obtainable, will be sent free on application to Gordon England (1929) Ltd., 32, South Molton Street, London, W.1. . . . . . Write for it.

PEACE & COMFORT IN AN ENGLAND BODY

Near the running board of an England Body is this small licence plate—the sign of a motorist who rides in peace and comfort.

E.B.10

Simple.... Strong.... Silent....
P·S·C Pressed Steel bodywork with the new principle of "one-piece" construction

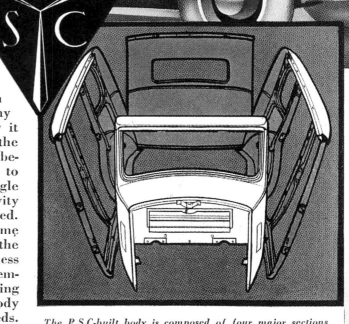

P.S.C pressed steel has delivered body-building from the complication of many separate parts. That is how it has been possible to scrap the old-fashioned wood frame between body and chassis and to build both together as a single rigid unit. The centre of gravity is lowered; safety increased. The dead weight of solid frame and supports is changed for the immense strength and lightness of P.S.C pressed steel members. Special sound deadening methods keep the whole body perfectly silent at all speeds.

MORRIS	AUSTIN
HILLMAN	WOLSELEY
ROVER	M.G.

are using P.S.C Pressed Steel

The P.S.C-built body is composed of four major sections as shown. These are strongly welded together to form one complete body. All the bits and pieces, the nuts and bolts and joints previously associated with car bodywork are thereby completely eliminated—and with them all rattle and squeak and looseness.

P.S.C MAKES POSSIBLE THE "ONE-PIECE" CAR

THE PRESSED STEEL COMPANY
OXFORD

A PRICELESS POSSESSION

"I CAN'T bear to see her go," said Barbara.

"You needn't," I replied manfully.

"But I shall hear," she protested tearfully.

"Not if you go to your bath and splash."

She bit her trembling lip.

"How you can do it I can't imagine."

"I am a man," I said simply.

"Poor darling Susan!" she gulped. "To think that I have washed her and—and greased her for the last time."

"Don't," I implored, "please don't go on. You will make me lose my grip on myself."

"As long as you don't lose your grip on her I don't mind," said Barbara.

"Enough!" I said harshly; "the time has come."

Barbara clung to me. "They will be kind to her, won't they? Make—make them promise."

"Of course—of course."

"And you'll tell them that her favourite oil is—"

I was pained. "What do you take me for?" I growled.

"I'm sorry," said Barbara penitently.

"Well," I said, bracing back my shoulders, "the longer I stay here talking to you the harder it—"

"Yes," said Barbara, "we must not shrink; but—but don't let them say anything too personal in her hearing."

"I will keep her engine running so that she can't hear."

"Is that wise," said Barbara, "or kind? It would be very painful for her if—I mean—"

"I see what you mean," I said tenderly and went down to the garage.

Like most ladies, Susan is usually rather a bad starter, but on this occasion half a turn of the handle set her purring—well, anyway, firing. That affected me strangely, but I would not give in. I lowered the muff over her eyes and navigated her down the drive. In spite of a nasty head-wind we arrived at the garage gallantly and drew up without a squeak.

"Good morning, Sir," said the sales manager. He had kind eyes.

"Good morning," I replied brightly—rather too brightly perhaps.

"Is this the—er—?

"Yes," I said hastily and disembarked. "Engine ticking over nicely—what?"

He winced. "Er—yes," he said; "shall we stop it for a moment?"

"Just as you like." I laughed casually. "I started her this morning with half a turn of the handle."

"Indeed, Sir? Self-starter out of action perhaps."

"Well—er—in a way, yes."

"Yes, Sir," he said sympathetically, "I know the way you mean."

I warmed towards this man. "She's been a wonderful little car," I said enthusiastically.

"Yes," he said, "she looks it."

"I've been all over the country in her. Up hills—"

"Really?"

"And down."

"Quite."

"Only last summer she took me all the way to Cornwall."

"And back?

"Well, no; as a matter of fact it was really I who brought her back, if you know what I mean."

"I know exactly, Sir."

"It was entirely my fault. I got so absorbed in the scenery one day that I forgot to give her her oil at luncheon."

"Ah! Then she is extravagant in oil?"

"Not extravagant, but—well—fond of it. I mean she doesn't throw it about or waste it or anything like that. She uses up every drop. I never grudge anything if it is really wanted."

"It is always nice," he observed, "to be generous if you can afford to be." Charming man!

"And how about petrol?" he proceeded.

"Well, of course petrol *is* her staple food."

"Eats petrol—just so. And—er—easy to steer?"

"Not so much easy as fascinating."

He nodded. "I understand, Sir," he said.

"I knew you would," I replied warmly.

"Have you ever had an accident in her?"

"Nothing fatal."

"Oh, well, that's something, isn't it?"

"Speaking as an owner-driver, I think it is everything."

There was a pause while we stood side by side admiring Susan.

"Tyres seem rather worn," he remarked at last.

"Yes. Of course speed does that."

"Or the wheels not being in track."

"Really? How very interesting! I never knew that."

"You have never had your wheels tested for track?"

"Never," I said proudly.

He smiled wanly. "Perhaps," he ventured, "we might give her engine a little run now?"

"She would enjoy it," I assented cordially. "No doubt you would like to see for yourself how easy she is to start."

"I should," he said, and went to the starting handle.

"No," I explained after a bit, "I don't think you have quite got hold of the idea. Let me show you— There! It's more of a knack than anything."

"Did it take you long to discover the knack?" he shouted.

I shook my head. He came very close to me.

"Does—she—always—make—that—noise?" he yelled.

I nodded happily. He rushed to the dashboard and switched her off.

"Yes," I went on chattily, "that sound is characteristic of her; so much so that our dog knows her from any other car on the road."

People have often doubted me when I have told them that, but I could see that he believed it.

"But then dogs have such sensitive ears," I concluded.

"So have I," he said.

"You are lucky," I said; but he didn't seem to agree. An awkward silence ensued.

"Well," I said, breaking it self-consciously, "what do you—er—?"

"Would it," he interposed mercifully, "be a question of part exchange?"

"I'm afraid not," I replied. "The fact is that I haven't got the other part."

He turned away. I could see that he was trying to master his feelings.

"Of course," he whispered at last, "these old cars really mean more to their owners than they do to us."

"You mean—?" I said, the light of a great truth dawning upon me.

"I do, Sir," he replied solemnly.

"Thank you," I said gripping his hand, "thank you. You have given me fresh courage."

"You will need it, Sir," he said gently and went back to his showroom.

Barbara was waiting for us when we got back.

"I had a presentiment," she said softly, "that they would not be worthy of her."

I got out and kissed her—Barbara. While I was doing it Susan stopped. Barbara sprang forward anxiously.

"She has only choked," I said.

"Of course," said Barbara—"with emotion. What is that dripping?"

I bent down and smelt. "Petrol," I said.

"No," said Barbara wistfully, "tears of joy," and proceeded to follow suit.

THE £498 CROSSLEY
is a very remarkable car

This 15.7 Coachbuilt Saloon, Standard Model, is a 'luxury-class' car in all respects save one—its price. It is a fine big roomy car, with adjustable front seat and ample accommodation for five. It is beautifully finished—cellulose without, leather upholstery within. Its springing is so perfect that it takes a very bad road indeed to disturb the peace of body of the most susceptible passenger. On steep hills it rejoices to show what its big-hearted engine can do. And its price, including full equipment, is but £498.

See also the 15.7 Coachbuilt De Luxe £575, and the Two-litre Sports.

CROSSLEY
15.7 SIX 20.9

London Distributors: HENLYS, *Henly House,* 385-387 *Euston* Road, *N.W.1*
and Devonshire House, Piccadilly, W.1
CROSSLEY MOTORS LTD., MANCHESTER

THE TEN-POUND CAR

SPRING is in the air and I have just bought a car for ten pounds. The garage from which I bought it being at the top of a hill, I drove it away myself.

It is quite a good car, and once you have tied the carburettor choke-lever back with string and reminded yourself to keep that part of the magneto-cable where the insulation has worn off away from any part of the vehicle and, more important, from any part of yourself, it really goes very well.

The trouble is though that things keep dropping off. On my very first run a floor-board suddenly disintegrated into three pieces and slid out of the bottom, leaving me poised perilously over naked pedals and bars of iron and a swiftly-moving road-surface. Before I could bring the machine to a standstill an empty petrol-can on the side, growing apparently weary of life, suddenly cast itself headlong overboard. Luckily a following lorry, endeavouring to avoid three simultaneous pieces of floorboard studded with nails, drove slap over the petrol-can and thus provided me with a substitute for the floor-board till I reached home.

The next thing to part company was a butterfly-nut from the wind-screen, which fell into the depths of the machinery. I haven't retrieved it yet, but now and then I hear it and feel it is nice to know it is not lost. I have temporarily replaced it with a nut from the back of the driver's seat, which has thus become a collapsible seat—a most convenient thing to have. The passenger's seat always was collapsible. When it is occupied it collapses backwards, but fortunately there is still the original floorboard on the rear part of the car. When it is vacant it collapses forward, striking the driver a shrewd and unexpected blow on the left elbow. The invariable result is a repercussion on the front right wing. This used to be awkward, but now that the valuable side-lamp on the wing has dropped off I don't mind so much, for once a wing is thoroughly crumpled fresh crumples don't show. I now call this wing the cauliflower ear.

The side-lamp, by the way, has finally been tied into the mouth of the horn. It fits beautifully and it is the only place where it will stay. For a while I tried it on the right wheel-hub, but it went round and round and made me look too like an occulting lighthouse that has moved inland for the summer. Even now it goes out for some reason every time I blow the horn on a right-hand corner.

Then there is a kind of tip-up tool-closet next the back-seat which suddenly falls down with a loud clatter and for no reason at all that I can discover. Probably it is mere temperament. Whenever it does this it cascades a jack, three spanners, an oil-can (empty after the fourth time) and two tyre-levers into the back with a noise like the delivering of a load of scrap-iron on a wooden roof. At first I used to pull up and go back along the road looking for what had dropped off. Indeed I once spent half-an-hour fitting somewhere into the car a piece of metal which I had found fifty yards back—only to discover next day that it had nothing to do with me or my car whatever, but belonged to somebody else's perambulator. It says a good bit for the car that I did fit it in, and that the works apparently went better after it.

But now I am no longer deceived by the tool-closet game, though other people, I fear, are not so accustomed to it. Only last week I had just drawn up to allow a racing-car to pass—I find this kinder—when off went my salvo of tools with a thunderous rattle. I was so busy re-stowing them that I did not notice for a little while that the racing-car had drawn up further on and the chauffeur was peering at his back-axle with a puzzled expression. Even then I did not understand what had happened, and went and helped him peer at it. I realised eventually; but I was not brave enough to tell him. He drove off sadly—and now he'll never know.

So far the only thing that hasn't fallen off in motion is a wheel. One did a week ago, but the car was standing still at the time. It was just after a dog had barked at it, but I think it must have been loose before that. Of course I am not counting the spare wheel which took a plunge at the top of a long straight hill leading down into a quiet village. I watched its progress with interest, but after what it did to that village I decided not to claim it. A pity, for it had been a good wheel in its day.

But I must not complain. I only paid ten pounds, and the man said I could re-sell it at the end of the season for the breaking-up price of five pounds. There however, he was quite wrong; the ten pounds I paid for it was really the breaking-up price. For, at the present rate of disintegration, by the end of the season I estimate that there will be nothing left of the thing.

1932

LOOK AT THE TREAD—
THAT'S FOR
GREATER SAFETY

INSIDE THERE'S
THE GUM-DIPPED
CORD — THAT'S FOR
MORE MILEAGE
FIRESTONE TYRES GIVE YOU BOTH

The Mark of Quality

Firestone

MADE IN ENGLAND
ON THE GREAT WEST ROAD NEAR LONDON

SPEED WITH SAFETY

SINGING ALONG IN A SINGER

All the joy and pleasures of motoring are completely realised in the wonderful SINGER "SIX." A stirring example of British motor supremacy. The spirit of the age expressed in a modern motor car. So supreme in its beauty and performance that it leaves all competitors far behind. To ride in the new SINGER "SIX" is an exhilarating experience which awaits you. Will you have a trial run? Behind the wheel you get the facts!

Equipment includes Triplex safety glass, chromium plating, wire wheels, bumpers, real leather upholstery, hydro-pneumatic shock-absorbers. SIX Saloon, £275. Super Six, £350. SINGER Dealers throughout the country will be pleased to give you a Demonstration. Please write for the " SIX " Catalogue to:—

SINGER & COMPANY, LTD., COVENTRY.
LONDON SHOWROOMS . . STRATTON HOUSE, PICCADILLY, W.1.

THIS IS BRITISH

THE PEDESTRIAN'S CHARTER

Mr. HERBERT MORRISON, Minister of Transport, has been taking the Press into his confidence, if not his counsels, on the subject of the regulations which he proposes to bring into force with the idea of making the highway safer for democracy.

WE pedestrians yet alive
　Bless the new rules (Mr. MORRISON'S),
And as long as we survive
　Shall "remember in our orisons"
One that in his mercy said:
"I could do with fewer dead."

His are not the first decrees
　In our favour promulgated;
None may knock us flat if he's
　Hopelessly inebriated;
All good drivers have this motto:
"Do not drive when you are blotto."

Motorists, if they would climb
　Over people, having done 'em in,
Must be sober at the time,
　Otherwise the cop will run 'em in;
And to this we now may add,
They must not be raving mad.

Soon I hope to walk about
　Feeling rather more eupeptic,
When a man can't lay me out
　Should his state be epileptic,
Nor may claim this lethal right
If he lacks the gift of sight.

And—what makes me more secure—
　Ere he puts me in the cart, he
Must on my behalf insure
　As an interested party;
He must pay for my repair
Or appease my orphaned heir.

Finally, the dangers which
　Cloud my daily life and dim it
Come, I hear—ay, there's the hitch—
　From the present legal limit;
And my faint heart will be healed
Once that peril is repealed.

Greatly comforted by that,
　I shall look for cars in plenty
Authorised to rush me at
　Sixty miles instead of twenty;
No more limbs for me to mend;
Just a swift and painless end.

'You dragged this man a hundred yards.'
'But only at thirty miles an hour.'

1933

Up and down the country motorists are driving the latest Hillmans . . . . learning what a difference "Cushioned Power" does make to motoring. The new **WIZARD** from **£280** gives the highest level of performance and comfort ever attained in its price class . . . with the new "Cyclonic" Induction giving vivid acceleration, astonishing power output and low running costs . . . . and there are three new full **7-SEATER WIZARDS** from **£350** . . . . The sturdy **MINX** 10/30 h.p. from **£159** is a big car in all but cost . . . . a light car with large car looks and performance.

Triplex Glass throughout (Windscreen on Minx Saloon, Wizard 5 and 7-seater saloons)

HILLMAN

WRITE FOR INTERESTING BROCHURES

Please address your enquiry to Dept. L.,
THE HILLMAN MOTOR CAR CO. LTD., COVENTRY. *London Showrooms and Export Dept.,* ROOTES LTD., DEVONSHIRE HOUSE, PICCADILLY, W.1.
London Service Station, Lodge Place, St. John's Wood Road.

OVERSEAS REPRESENTATIVES.

EUROPE: *Mr. A. L. S. Cope,*	AUSTRALIA & NEW ZEALAND:	SOUTH AFRICA: *Mr. John Good, Rootes Ltd.,*	INDIA, BURMA & CEYLON:	SOUTH AMERICA:
Rootes Ltd., Devonshire House,	*Mr. C. E. Blayney, Rootes Ltd.,*	*Barclays Bank Chbrs. Cfr Strand and Loop*	*Mr. H. H. Lilley, Rootes Ltd.,*	*Rootes Argentina S.A.*
Piccadilly, London, W.1.	*Herald Buildings, Pitt St., Sydney.*	*Streets, Capetown (or P.O. Box 2417.*	*72, Park Street, Calcutta.*	*Callao 1111, Buenos Aires.*

Every Hillman owner should read "Modern Motoring," price 1d. monthly, obtainable through any newsagent 6/6 per annum post free

APPLE GIVES A LIFT

THE other day Apple was bowling along the main road in his wonderful ten-horse, ten-pound tin-can car, about which he was telling you some little while ago, and which he has now christened Mélange (by Ingenuity out of Scrapheap). On second thoughts perhaps "bowling" is hardly the word. Things were rattling and clattering underneath, there was a wobbly front wheel, and inside the bonnet all the tappets were clicking away like a mothers' meeting with loose dentures. One cylinder was missing, and so was part of the clutch-pedal, while more vital parts were tied up with string. In short, the general effect of Apple's progress was like the White Knight going into battle in full marching order, and Apple was happy.

Not so those on his route. Children and animals ran in terror into the hedges some while before Mélange came in sight and cowered there as she passed. Even deaf old ladies hobbled indoors, their fingers to their ears; startled men in shirt-sleeves peered apprehensively from windows, and garage hands removed their hats in reverent awe. Looking back now, Apple feels he may have exaggerated a trifle, but anyhow it was in this sort of atmosphere that he passed along the roads, leaving behind quite another sort of atmosphere—pale blue and smelling of burnt waste and overheated metal.

Then the incredible thing happened—that is, the other incredible thing, the first being that Apple had already achieved twenty-eight miles of his journey to London without either a break-down of the machinery or a break-up of the car: *Apple was hailed for a lift.*

Now Apple had already offered lifts to two weary walkers and had received the courteous answer, before they trudged on, that, no thanks, they were in a hurry. So in this particular case Apple could hardly believe his eyes and ears. He drew up smartly at the signal, however, having recently lost a complete mudguard off the back from ignoring a wayside shout which was really helpful and informative, but which he took to be humorous and derogatory.

Having examined the back of Mélange and found all present and correct, he examined the face of the young man and noted that the fellow was not myopic and appeared to be in his right mind. And yet he had apparently stopped Apple's car for a lift. "Do you *really* want a lift?" inquired Apple, sadly shaking his head at the rash follies of youth.

"Thanks so much. To Kingston—if you're going as far."

Apple looked sharply at him, but it was said in all sincerity. Trying to speak with conviction Apple said he was going through Kingston, even to London. Whereupon the fellow opened the door, climbed in, climbed out again, picked up the door from the road, and climbed back bringing it with him. Apple, who after bitter experience had left Mélange's engine limping, slapped her smartly on the gear-box. She ground her teeth back at him and they were off.

The young man, Apple discovered, was one of those who pay, so to speak, for their lift by being terribly pleasant about their benefactor's car. He chatted about the old death-waggon in such an approving fashion that Apple again wondered whether he really was quite right in the head. However, the fellow continued to lay it on about the acceleration and the sweet running and even the charming little blue sparks which in moments of emotional stress play round Mélange's dynamo switch, till Apple could only assume that he didn't often travel in cars.

When at last he said something quite too flattering about silent running—having to raise his voice and bellow in Apple's ear in order to put it across—Apple asked him point-blank if he were a driver himself. The young man replied that his job didn't allow him much time for riding in cars, that he had never owned one, nor indeed ever driven one in his life.

To this discovery, Apple, being but human, instantly responded. (Mélange, being something more than human, also responded—by ceasing to spit in an offensive manner and beginning to fire on the fourth cylinder, hitherto a mere passenger in the boat.) He at once became the complete driver. He lounged impressively back in his seat, instead of sitting crouched up over the wheel as one fearing the worst; he steered with one hand only; he trod in Brooklands fashion on the accelerator, and he even waved back an impatient push-cyclist, who, after squeaking a nasty little horn at him from behind, had been about to pass.

With the added cylinder Mélange began to put on speed. She even purred. Other cars no longer overtook so quickly that Apple didn't know they'd come till they'd gone. Apple himself even overtook a Ford, though, glancing back, he noticed that it seemed to be drawing in to the side for a halt anyway. He raised the speed still further and his passenger politely pretended to hold his hat on. This led Apple to talk largely about a Bowls-Royster he had once passed on Reigate Hill, omitting, however, to add that it had been going in the opposite direction.

Nearing Kingston, Apple became the absolute Speed Demon. He went really fast and was glad to notice his companion was displaying signs of nervousness by peering out over the side at the flying roadway. Apple thereupon enlarged upon "Speed," explaining that, to those who weren't accustomed to it, it was a little terrifying at first, but that when one was close to the ground one appeared to be going faster than one really was. Then, by way of impressing his passenger further, Apple called upon Mélange for a final burst. During this grand climax the speedometer touched forty two or three times and the car touched the road about five or six. All this unnerved Apple quite a bit, but he didn't dare show it in front of his companion, who had probably never experienced such a speed before.

In Kingston, Apple drew up with a flourish at the spot requested and his passenger got out. Just before driving on, Apple, feeling very condescending, told him he needn't have been nervous; such speed was really nothing. The fellow, now looking much relieved, and very grateful, apparently, for both the lift and his life, explained that he had been a little anxious about one of Apple's front wheels, which seemed to be loose, but that it didn't matter now. Mere speed didn't worry him, he added as he moved off; he was used to it. Though, funnily enough, he'd never driven a car, he was quite used to aeroplane speeds, which were, he believed, a trifle higher; for his job was, he modestly added, that of pilot in National Airway Services, Ltd . . .

Apple drove away thoughtfully, only stopping when well round the corner to borrow some more string and repair his front wheel.

THE DRIVER: 'What do you think of these little things?'
THE PASSENGER: 'Make topping ash-trays.'

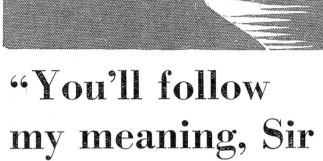

"You'll follow my meaning, Sir

When it comes to washing a car down with water—well it's not a job anyone would do for pleasure—a gentleman will shirk it, Sir, and no wonder. Every car that's cleaned by its owner ought to be cleaned with Karpol. And then it's a job anyone can do, the dirt and grease and fresh tar coming off soft and easy and the polish fetching up fine. No one minds a job like that. And the car gets cleaned regular and the coachwork gets what's due to it. It's the only way it will, Sir."

RECKITT'S

KARPOL

Cleans coachwork without water

RECKITT & SONS LTD. HULL AND LONDON

THE OWNER-DRIVER AND THE MAGISTRATE

A FABLE

NOW there was a certain Owner-Driver who, after making a Night of It, was Piloting his Chariot along a ticklish Stretch of the Highway when he was Accosted by a Custodian in Blue, who Asseverated that the Owner-Driver was under the Influence of Bacchic Juices.

And in due course the Owner-Driver was Arraigned at an appropriate Palace of Justice, where there were Three Charioteers in Like Case waiting to Plead; and the Owner-Driver listened with Peculiar Interest as in Turn they pointed out to the Magistrate that it was all a Mistake, since each one Severally had imbibed but a Modicum of Ordinary Wine or a small Measure or two of an Innocuous Malt Liquor, and that their Erratic Driving was not to be Ascribed to Indiscreet Potations but to the Toxic Effect (1) of Cocaine at the dentist's, (2) of Bella Donna at the oculist's and (3) of Anxiety over the Chronic Neuritis of a Favourite Aunt, respectively.

Now it happened that on his Way to the Palace of Justice the Magistrate had escaped Death from a Straight Six only by a Display of Agility well-nigh Incredible in one of his Years, and had besides been Dubbed a Jay-Walker; and as he took his seat to Dispense Justice he was not in the Mood to allow his Judgment to be Deflected by Mistaken Tolerance, so that the Pleadings of the Three Charioteers cut very little Ice with him, and he told them that only by a great Effort could he Dissuade himself from Incarcerating them and Let them Off with a Swingeing Fine.

When it came to the Turn of the Owner-Driver to take his Stand at the Bar of Justice he was Very Downcast; for the Tale that he had been going to Tell seemed Wholly Inadequate now that the more Ingenious Pleadings of the others had been of No Avail. Moreover the Cynical stare of the Magistrate Short-Circuited his Resource and Blew Out the Fuse of his Invention. But as he stood with a Blank Expression there Suddenly came to his mind the long-neglected Apostrophe of his Sunday-School Monitress on the Value of Veracity, and without knowing Quite what he did he Committed himself to the Desperate Expedient of telling the Truth, saying:—

"I must Admit that I had been Wassailing. I was, Indubitably, One over the Eight, and I am glad that the timely Intervention of the Custodian checked my Career before I had Winged an innocent Pedestrian."

For some moments the Magistrate pondered over this Defence before he replied Sternly: "In all these Cases I am Accustomed to the Wildest Prevarication and Hard Swearing. I have no Reason to Assume that you are an Exception. What is the latent Subtlety of your novel Defence is altogether Beyond me, but as a matter of Routine and Consistency I must Refuse to believe a Word you Say. I am Therefore forced to the Conclusion that you were in Fact, Stone Cold Sober, and That Being So, I must reluctantly Discharge you without a Stain on your Character."

Moral: In Peculiar Circumstances the Truth may be found to Prevail.

Probable scene in the proximity of police trap, now that the practice of warning motorists has been declared illegal.

SNIPE "80" SPORTS SALOON £550. *Triplex Glass throughout*

The choice of the experienced motorist

HUMBER

HUMBER LIMITED, COVENTRY. *London Showrooms & Export Dept.:* ROOTES LTD., DEVONSHIRE HOUSE, PICCADILLY, W.1.
London Service Depot: Somerton Road, Cricklewood, N.W.2.

OVERSEAS REPRESENTATIVES: *Australia and New Zealand:* Mr. C. E. Blayney, Rootes Ltd., Herald Buildings, Pitt Street, Sydney. *South Africa:* Mr. John Good, Rootes Ltd., Barclays Bank Chambers, C r Strand and Loop Streets, Capetown (or P.O. Box 2417). *India, Burma and Ceylon:* Mr. H. H. Lilley, Rootes Ltd., 72, Park Street, Calcutta. *South America:* Rootes Argentina S.A. Callao, 1111 Buenos Aires. *Europe:* Mr. A. L. S. Cope, Rootes Ltd., Devonshire House, Piccadilly, London, W.1.

EVERY HUMBER OWNER SHOULD READ "MODERN MOTORING." PRICE 4d. MONTHLY, OBTAINABLE THROUGH ANY NEWSAGENT. 6/6 PER ANNUM POST FREE

Time is never lost
through failure of the lights —
Chloride Batteries are installed !

Behind the scenes in a modern factory there is often a Chloride Battery. The works economist has thought of the time lost through failure of the lights. He has cancelled it, once and for all, with a Chloride Battery. It is there to hoard up light, to put it by for the sudden emergency.

The Chloride Battery is deliberately chosen to fill places of trust. In ships and shops, and in hospitals and cinemas. With so much faith put in it, you may not doubt the Chloride Battery to be any but the supreme battery of the world.

for
**HOSPITALS
SHIPS
FACTORIES
CINEMAS, STORES
AND COUNTRY HOUSES**

Chloride
STORAGE BATTERIES

THE CHLORIDE ELECTRICAL STORAGE COMPANY LTD., CLIFTON JUNCTION, NEAR MANCHESTER
London Office at 137 Victoria Street, S.W.1

SONG OF THE MECHANIC

IF your engine should stop when you're
    miles from a shop
    And you think you've a choked
      carburettor,
Or you find that the hood doesn't work as
    it should
    And your seat's getting wetter and
      wetter;
If the dynamo squeaks or the petrol-tank
    leaks,
    Your language need not be volcanic,
For you very well know you have only
      to go
    And ring up a motor-mechanic.

If your pistons should seize or your water-
    pipe freeze,
    Or you've got too much play in your
      steering;
If your glands come unpacked or your
    brakes will not act
    When down a steep hill you're careering;
If you puncture your tyres or your engine
    misfires,
    Or your mascot proves untalismanic—
Well, you very well know you have only
      to go
    And ring up a motor-mechanic.

If you car should capsize and you find
    with surprise
    That you're buried completely beneath
      it,
Matters might have been worse, so it's
    foolish to curse
    And perhaps to the devil bequeath it;
For on hearing such names it will burst
    into flames,
    But there's no need to get in a panic,
As you very well know you have only to go
    And ring up a motor-mechanic.

OVERWROUGHT WIFE. "Don't stand there like an idiot! I thought you always got underneath to see
what's the matter."

In Sports — *it's* Polo

in Tyres *it's* Goodyear

The Heavy Duty All-Weather Tread tyre by Goodyear is the finest tyre that it is possible to make. We built it for people who are accustomed to enjoy the finest. It is extravagantly made—actually a much better tyre than normal need requires.

In building it we had safety as well as beauty, silence, and endurance in mind; we gave it Double Safety—safety against skids; safety against bursts.

Every day the reputation of the Heavy Duty tyre by Goodyear is growing as word of its worth is more widely spread.

BRITISH MADE — TO AN ENTIRELY NEW STANDARD OF QUALITY

AN IMPROVED MODEL
To the Motor Taxation Officer

DEAR SIR,—Thank you so much for your form R.F.1A (revised August, 1929) and for your kind inquiries about my mechanically-propelled road vehicle. Strictly speaking, of course, it is not nearly so mechanically propelled as you seem to imagine. Generally it is towed. But we'll let that pass.

I hope you don't mind my writing fully on this matter. One has to be so careful what one puts on a buff form, and you haven't given me much space. For instance, your question 5, under the heading STATE HERE, reads, you will remember: "What alterations, if any, have been made affecting registration particulars since last declaration . . .?" And to answer a momentous question like that you give a half-a-line—just space enough to reply "Yes" or "No." It is not enough for a case like mine.

If you were to ask me what alterations have not taken place I might have squeezed the particulars into the allotted space. But since you require me to name the alterations I must sketch briefly in this friendly letter exactly how my mechanically-propelled road vehicle has been improved.

Your records will tell you what my car was like originally. A sound job which earned its designer a knighthood. Of course I would not have tampered with a work which had earned a knighthood unless I had acted under advice. It was good advice, tendered disinterestedly by men who had forgotten more about motors than the knightly designer has ever learned. They told me so themselves. And, if they hadn't been rewarded with knighthoods, that was only because they shunned publicity.

That is why my dashboard looks so dashed interesting. Inquisitive passengers have electrocuted themselves by touching things on my dashboard. I admit it is all a little difficult to the uninitiated. I myself have occasionally switched on the windscreen-wiper and got dance-music from Paris Radio. And once, I remember, in thick traffic I got Koenigswusterhausen.

But generally I specialise in useful gadgets. I believe in Safety First, for when one is alone in a car one can't be too careful. I am alone in the car a good deal, because my friends too believe in Safety First. I don't blame them, but it does throw a fellow on his own resources.

Think of the danger of fire, for instance. Petrol is highly inflammable, and to avoid going up in smoke before my time I carry an extinguisher. This is a chromium-plated gadget, a little like a vacuum-cleaner, which squirts some noisome fluid on the seat of the conflagration.

But a gadget fastened on the foot-board outside would only be effective if I too happened to be outside when the conflagration started. Otherwise the delay in jumping out and running round might be fatal. So I've had a second extinguisher installed inside.

The possibility of fire led to another consideration. People have been trapped in saloons. It's a curious thing, but saloon-doors are always swinging open; yet as soon as a fire breaks out they jam. I know just how to deal with an emergency like that, for a letter in the Press showed me the way out—at least I hope it will be the way out. He suggested that all users of closed cars should carry axes. According to him, axes should be fixed as standard.

He also suggested that, if I only attached a bell to the dash, my car might be mistaken for a fire-engine. This would be a useful extra, because even confirmed jay-walkers take notice of a bell.

Of course I have horns in plenty. Each of my technical advisers advocates a different kind of horn, so I have fitted one of each. Almost an orchestra, in fact. If I had two more horns I might be able to play the National Anthem. This is worth striving after. At the first bars of the National Anthem pedestrians would stiffen to attention; and it would be comparatively easy to miss pedestrians who stood to attention.

I have repainted the mechanically-propelled road vehicle in two shades of brown, instead of maroon as formerly. The drop-head coupé has been dismantled and it is now a two-seater (with dickey). The off-side rear wing is buckled as a result of a mishap when the bus was really being a mechanically-propelled vehicle, and I have added an orange fog-lamp and an anti-glare visor.

When we come to the engine there are further changes. I seem to have the same number of plugs sticking out of the cylinder-head, so I think it is a fair assumption that I still have four cylinders—although only three of them do any mechanical propulsion. But a carburettor, a magneto and a battery have been grafted on the original stock. These were transferred from (*a*) an Italian, (*b*) a French and (*c*) an American car respectively. The nationality of my own car is thus a trifle obscure. I hope this will make no difference to my licence. It is practically the same car.

    Cheerio,

        GEORGE HOPKINS

    P.S.—We are buying a new mascot on Monday, but we have not quite decided on the design. Will wire particulars as soon as available.

A MASCOT ROMANCE

Rolls-Royce Ltd., makers of the Best Car in the World, use and recommend this Peerless Lubricant

1935

The New De Luxe Ford is all its name implies, a light car of a new class, manufactured at Dagenham. It is distinguished in any company, a super-product, so fashioned that the most critical inspection and exacting road-trial will evoke a positive stream of admiring superlatives. Its first cost, taxation, insurance, running and maintenance, are all in tune with the inclination toward sane spending, sensible economy.

"There Is No Comparison!"

DE LUXE FORD SALOON, £135.   DE LUXE FORD DOUBLE-ENTRANCE SALOON, £145.

Literature on Request   :   Prices at Works   :   Dealers Everywhere

FORD MOTOR COMPANY LIMITED, DAGENHAM, ESSEX.   SHOWROOMS: 88 REGENT STREET, LONDON, W.I.

THE OPEN ROAD

"LET us go," I said, "to Batchworth."

"Or Filton?" suggested my wife. Phyllis is like that.

"Batchworth!" I repeated firmly.

We set out for Filton.

There was a hint of frost in the air and the sun was shining vigorously. A wonderful day—a day to inspire poets; a day among days; in short, a day for the Open Road.

"A Sunny Morn, an Open Road, and Thou
     Beside me singing in the limousine,
And Filtonwards is Paradise enow,"

I chanted.

"Only it's not a limousine and I'm not singing," Phyllis pointed out. I sighed. Against my wife's passion for accuracy mere poetic licence stood no chance at all. Suddenly Phyllis clutched my arm and pointed ahead along the road.

"Hullo! What's that fellow getting so excited about?" I muttered, bringing the car to a standstill.

A red-faced man, wearing, among other things, a red muffler, was waving a red flag two feet from my radiator.

"I wave this flag," said the red-faced man, "because there is a trifling obstruction hereabouts. It was nice of you to stop. I thought at first that you hadn't noticed me—we all make our little mistakes at times, don't we? Ah! I see the road is clear now. Won't you move on?"

That at any rate was the general idea lying behind his remarks.

Cautiously we crawled past two hundred yards of chaos.

Once more the Open Road.

I settled back and pressed the accelerator.

"This is undoubtedly the life," I cried as we rounded a pretty little bend. Then very quickly I applied all the brakes I had.

"Didn't you see the warning, dear?" inquired Phyllis.

"Oh, I *saw* it all right," I lied airily.

"All the same it is an extraordinary thing that whenever I come anywhere near a level-crossing the infernal thing shuts up."

"The last one was open, dear; don't you remember?" said Phyllis.

In silence I reached for my cigarette-case. Phyllis resents hyperbole.

"One of the advantages of the Batchworth road," I remarked at length, "is that there are no level-crossings."

The point, however, was not taken.

Not more than three minutes later a solitary tank-engine fussed by. After a while it came back, having apparently taken the wrong turning. I caught a glimpse of the driver; he did not look upset. We waited anxiously, half expecting it would return. That was all for the present, however, and an old man hobbled slowly down from a signal-box and opened one of the gates. Later he opened the other and we passed across.

"We are all right now for a bit," I said as I opened out. "The next village is five miles off."

Wide, straight and magnificently empty it lay ahead of us—the Open Road.

"What-ho!" I cried exultantly.

"Let her rip!" urged Phyllis, catching something of my boyish enthusiasm.

I let her rip.

Suddenly the road narrowed. Phyllis shut her eyes.

"Didn't you see the warn—" she began when immediate disaster had been averted.

"Yes," I snapped, truthfully this time, "I did. But I did *not* expect that two-thirds of the traffic of the county would choose just this particular bit of tarmac to play on."

We followed the swaying stern of a steam-waggon for a quarter of a mile or so, overtook it and slid gently into place behind a pantechnicon. The pantechnicon stopped abruptly. So did we—only still more abruptly. Behind us a long line of cars appeared mysteriously out of the blue and stopped also.

"Batchworth must be looking delightful to-day," I murmured, leisurely filling a pipe. "Do you remember that lunch they gave us there once—at 'The Swan', wasn't it?"

Phyllis changed the subject hastily. "I suppose the road is up again," she said.

"That," I replied cuttingly, "is not impossible."

By-and-by the driver of the pantechnicon climbed down and restarted his engine. On we went.

Five miles to Filton, and—the Open Road. Hope stirred in my breast. We should make it yet. I felt like a hero in a film. The miles flew by.

"This sort of thing is too good to last," I grunted.

It was. The road suddenly swarmed with sheep. In the distance were cows. Battalions of them.

Somehow or other we circumnavigated the sheep. We also passed the cows. Beyond the cows there was a corner. Beyond the corner were two policemen.

"Your licence, Sir, if you please," said one of them, peering in at the window.

While he was examining my papers the cows came by—then the sheep.

We went on.

"Is this Filton?" Phyllis asked in a disappointed tone.

"It is," I replied curtly. "Don't you like it?"

"It's rather crowded," she answered.

"It is," I said.

"Next time we'll go by Batchworth, shall we?"

"Next time," I retorted darkly, "we will go by train."

MOTORIST (*who is lost*): 'Is this the road to St. Ives?'
YOKEL: 'Dunno.'
MOTORIST: 'Is that the road to Willingham?'
YOKEL: 'Dunno.'
MOTORIST: 'Well, can you tell me which is the road to Cottenham?'
YOKEL: 'Dunno.'
MOTORIST (*exasperated*): 'Well, you don't seem to know much.'
YOKEL: 'Maybe not; but I ain't lost.'

your

GUARANTEE

of

safety

THIS IS TO CERTIFY
that your brakes have
this day been fitted with
FERODO BRAKE LININGS
manufactured by Ferodo Limited
Front Brakes ✓ *Rear Brakes* ✓

FERODO
GUARANTEE

Name and address of Garage
Jones Garages,
High St. Midtown,
Date *28ᵗʰ Jan '33*
Please turn over

Think of the occasions — every
motorist encounters them — when
your brakes saved you. If such an
emergency arose today, would they serve
you as well? Is their grip sure and even? Are they
as efficient as on the day the car was new? Or are you
taking a risk—the biggest risk a motorist can take?
If there is any doubt — have your brakes tested today.
And if they need relining — specify FERODO. Get the
FERODO Guarantee. For it, too, is an essential safety
precaution — proof positive that your brakes have been
brought to the highest possible pitch of efficiency.

You will find the FERODO Guarantee on the steering wheel when
you collect your car. It guarantees
that FERODO Brake Linings have
been fitted. And that is the
strongest guarantee you can possibly have that the brakes are now
contributing their utmost to your
motoring safety.

99 TIMES OUT OF 100~IT'S YOUR BRAKES THAT COUNT

FERODO

for safe braking

REGD. TRADE MARK
FERODO FERODO LIMITED CHAPEL-EN-LE-FRITH

THE ROAD TO HAUTBOIS

IT was clear that I had gone wrong somewhere. Ten minutes' driving in what appeared to be a deliberately-designed maze of by-roads had convinced me of that. There seemed to be an extraordinary number of lanes in this part of Norfolk—many more, I could have sworn, than had been discovered by the Ordnance Survey. Not that I had my map with me; as usual, I had left it at home. It was all most annoying, because I really did want to get to Hautbois that afternoon, and I had no idea whether I was going north or south when the lane gave another twist and revealed a road-mender doing something with a pick.

I stopped the car and said, "Excuse me, but can you tell me the way to Hautbois?"

I was a stranger to Norfolk and the language spoken there, so, following the light of nature and the dictates of an expensive education in French, I pronounced the word as (possibly) the original Norman conquerors pronounced it—certainly as a modern Frenchman would. I realise now that I was asking for trouble.

In reply to my question the road-mender put an enormous hand behind his ear. Thinking he was deaf, I switched off the engine and shouted into his cupped hand, "Am a right for Hautbois?"

He withdrew a foot or two, grinned and said, "Nor I ain't 'ard of 'earin' neither, bor; but weer was it you said?"

"Hautbois," I said, still in my best French, but feeling that something was wrong about this conversation.

"Never 'eard of it," he answered briefly.

"Oh, come," I said, "that won't do. You live here, don't you?"

"Ah," he said, "I live 'ere all right, bor. Forty year or more."

"Well," I said, "the place I want to go to is within five miles of us, so you must know it."

"What did you call it?" he said again.

I began to feel inexpressibly a fool. It seemed that the correct pronunciation of the word had been forgotten by the natives and that I was condemned to go through all possible variants in order to make my meaning clear.

"I want to go to Hautbois," I said, only this time I pronounced it "Hotboys."

He shook his head.

"Hortboys," I said.

"There ain't no such place," he answered calmly.

"Oboe," I suggested miserably, with faint memories of orchestras.

A gleam of laughter came into his eyes. "Seems you don't rightly know *weer* you want to get to, bor," he said.

"I do know really," I said earnestly, "but to tell the truth I can't pronounce it and I've forgotten my map; but I'll tell you what I'll do," I added, "I'll write it down—no, I haven't got anything to write with. Oh, this is the limit! I must find the place somehow. There simply can't be more than a dozen ways of pronouncing a short word like this."

"Well, bor," he said, "you say it all the ways you can think of an' I'll tell you when I 'ears un."

Feeling that I was living in a nightmare, but determined to see the business through, I drew a deep breath and embarked on a list of possible pronunciations.

"Listen," I said, "I want to go to Outbor, or Outboys, or Otboys, or Houtboys, or Hotboys, or Horbuss, or Habbuss, or Orbuss, or Hubbuss, or—"

"Oh," he said, "I've got it now—Hubbis; that's what you mean. Straight on, bor, for 'alf-a-mile, and then turn right weer the road forks. You can't miss it." He chuckled. "Hubbis," he said pityingly, "that's what you meant."

But when I got to Hautbois and explained to my friend what had made me so late he merely said, "My dear fellow, why didn't you *spell* the word? You'd have saved yourself a lot of trouble."

Well, yes, I suppose I could have done that.

Have you seen the new  LIGHT TWENTY

1935

A joy to drive with...

THE NEW ESSO PETROLS give you a new thrill in acceleration, more miles per gallon, and better climbing than ever. They are a revelation in anti-knock. Esso Ethyl, for example, gives knockless running in engines of the highest compression, and astonishing top-gear performance in all cars.

ESSO ETHYL · ESSO BENZOL MIXTURE · ESSO HIGH TEST

ESSO

QUALITY PETROLS

For lubrication use Essolube motor oil

ANGLO-AMERICAN OIL COMPANY, LTD., WESTMINSTER, LONDON, S.W.1 *Established 1888*

THE BEST LAID SCHEMES

A contemporary declares that the side-car stands unrivalled as a matchmaker. It would seem, however, that opinion on the subject is not unanimous.

WE motored together, the maiden and I,
 And I was delighted to take her,
For, frankly, I wanted my side-car to try
 Its skill as a little matchmaker;
Though up to that time I had striven my best,
 I'd more than a passing suspicion
The spark I was anxious to light in her
 breast
 Still suffered from faulty ignition.

We started betimes in the promptest of styles
 For scenes that were rustic and quiet;
I opened the throttle; we ate up the miles
 (A truly exhilarant diet);
Till sharply, as over a common we went,
 Gorse-clad (or it may have been heather),
The engine stopped short with a tactful
 intent
 To leave the young couple together.

'Twas instinct (I take it) directing my course
 That named as my first occupation
A fruitless endeavour to track to its source
 The cause of this sudden cessation;
And so I had tinkered with tools for a space
 Ere I thought of my favourite poet,
And said to myself, "Lo! the time and the
 place
 And the loved one in unison; go it."

I might have remembered man seldom
 appears
 Alluring in look or in manner
With a smut on his nose, oleaginous ears
 And frenziedly clutching a spanner;
Though down by the cycle I fell to my knees
 And ported my heart for inspection,
I only received for my passionate pleas
 A curt and conclusive rejection.

THE FLIRT.

THE MOTOR PERIL

DEAR MR. PUNCH,—I am venturing to write to you because I feel sure that there must be among your readers many ladies like myself whose country walks have been altogether spoilt by these dreadful motors. My own pleasure in such gentle exercise as I can take was utterly ruined until quite recently. There is no joy in taking a stroll with your life in your hand, as one may say; and having at last found a remedy for this state of things I am anxious to convey the knowledge to my fellow-sufferers without delay.

It was really Jugg who suggested it to me, though quite unconsciously. He is a *most* respectable man, and I always employ him when I have to drive to the station or to pay calls at a distance. Even when he sold his nice quiet horse and took to a motor-car I felt I could not give him up, for his wife—a *very* steady young woman—was our cook for several years, and was married from our house, and I am god-mother to their eldest child.

Well, a few weeks ago Jugg was driving me to meet a train when we overtook a flock of sheep. Though he knew we had not much time to spare he at once slowed down and proceeded most cautiously till we were safely past. I commended him for his prudence and he replied, "Well, Ma'am, we have to be careful with them; you see it'd cost me ten pounds if I was to run into a sheep."

I was thinking over his remark and wondering why a motorist should be fined ten pounds for killing a sheep and, as I had seen in the paper, only five pounds for killing a major-general, when the inspiration came! That very afternoon I went to Miss Pinks, my dressmaker, a very intelligent woman, and propounded my scheme. She adopted the idea with enthusiasm, and in less than a fortnight sent home a garment in which I can take my walks in perfect safety.

It is made of a light woollen cloth closely resembling astrakhan, and when I stand or walk it looks like an ordinary cloak; but it is so cleverly contrived that at the first sound of a motor in the lane I have only to stoop forward and at once a hood slips over my head, with two ears standing up in a most natural manner; while at the same time the skirt divides slightly at the back and a short tail appears, completing the resemblance to a harmless necessary sheep.

If I do not desire actually to put my hands on the ground I can turn to the hedge and pretend to nibble the grass on the bank. Wherever I choose to place myself I am *safe*. Cars, lorries and even motor-cycles draw aside and pass me slowly and with the greatest care. My walks are once more a source of innocent and healthful enjoyment; and I feel it a duty as well as a pleasure to pass on the suggestion to others.

I am, dear Mr. Punch,
    Your constant reader,
    MATILDA PARKES

P.S. I enclose a sketch, though I cannot draw well.

1936

· · · · · as LIVELY as a Daimler

Daimler smoothness, Daimler silence, Daimler elegance have become a tradition. Now there is a new generation of Daimlers with all these qualities plus an exhilarating liveliness, an unsuspected turn of speed.

OWNER-DRIVER CARS	
Fifteen - - -	£465
Light Twenty - -	£675
Light Straight Eight -	£995

CHAUFFEUR-DRIVEN LIMOUSINES	
Six Cylinder - -	£795
Straight Eight -	£1450

DAIMLER FLUID FLYWHEEL TRANSMISSION

BUY A CAR MADE IN ENGLAND   THE DAIMLER CO. LTD., COVENTRY

301 M·P·H
SIR MALCOLM CAMPBELL
CHOSE
WAKEFIELD
PATENT
Castrol
MOTOR OIL
FOR HIS ROLLS-ROYCE ENGINE

C·C·WAKEFIELD & CO·LTD·WAKEFIELD·HOUSE·CHEAPSIDE·LONDON·E·C·2

LOVE IN A CAR

"I have personal knowledge of marriages resulting from motor-car courtships."—The HON. C. S. ROLLS—*Daily Express*

WHEN Reginald asked me to drive in his car
    I knew what it meant for us both,
For peril to love-making offers no bar,
    But fosters the plighting of troth.
To the tender occasion I hastened to rise,
    So bought a new frock on the strength
      of it,
Some china-blue chiffon—to go with my
      eyes—
    And wrapped up my head with a length
      of it.

"Get in," said my lover, "as quick as you can!"
    He wore a black smear on his face,
And held out the hand of a rough artisan
    To pilot me into my place.
Like the engine my frock somehow seemed to
      mis-fire,
    For Reginald's manner was querulous,
But after some fuss with the near hind-wheel
      tyre
    We were off at a pace that was perilous.

"There's Brown just behind, on his second-
      hand brute,
    He thinks it can move, silly ass!"
Said Reggie with venom, "Ha! Ha! let him
      hoot,
    I'll give him some trouble to pass."
My service thenceforth was by Reggie
      confined
    (He showed small compunction in suing
      it)
To turning to see how far Brown was behind,
    But not to let Brown see me doing it.

Brown passed us. We dined off his dust for a
      league—
    It really was very poor fun—
Till, our car showed symptoms of heat and
      fatigue,
    Reggie had to admit he was done.
To my soft consolation scant heed did he pay,
    But with taps was continually juggling,
And his words, "Will you keep your dress
      further away?"
    Put a stop to this incipient smuggling.

"He'd never have passed me alone," Reggie
      sighed,
    "The car's extra heavy with you."
"Why ask me to come?" I remarked. He
      replied,
    "I thought she'd go better with two."
When I touched other topics, forbearingly
      meek,
    From his goggles the lightnings came
      scattering,
"What chance do you give me of placing this
      squeak,"
    He hissed, "when you keep up that
      chattering?"

At that, I insisted on being set down
    And returning to London by train,
And I vowed fifty times on my way back to
      town
    That I never would see him again.
Next week he appeared and implored me to
      wed,
    With a fondly adoring humility.
"The car stands between us," I rigidly said.
    "I've sold it!" he cried with agility.

His temples were sunken, enfeebled his
      frame,
    There was white in the curls on his crest;
When he spoke of our ride in a whisper of
      shame
    I flew to my home on his breast.
By running sedately I'm certain that Love
    To such passion would never have carried
      us,
Which settles the truth of the legend above—
    It was really the motor-car married us.

AS ONE MOTORIST TO ANOTHER

I AM delighted to note that the Automobile Association is approaching the Minister of Transport with a view to inventing some signal by which, in a situation of emergency, one motorist may stop another; for I have myself been advocating the need of such a convention for years.

I have gone so far indeed as to recommend that the compulsory equipment of all cars should include a kind of small cannon which would fire very soft rubber balls and over-ripe fruit with sufficient force to register a direct hit up to about fifty yards without doing damage. To ensure that the use of such a tempting engine would be confined to moments of genuine crisis, it would have to be clearly understood that any promiscuous pooping-off for the sheer fun of the thing would inevitably result in a fine of five pounds. This should be an adequate check on high spirits. The railway companies have found it so, for in practice only very rich people habitually pull the alarm-cord, attractive proposition though it be.

What the A.A. has chiefly in mind, of course, is the present difficulty of intimating to the fellow in front that one of his back wheels has just rolled into the ditch, that most of his doors are open, that he has at last fallen asleep over the helm, and that in general he is the victim of circumstances which may at any moment involve him in a serious accident. The element of time being all-important in such cases, the A.A. rightly deprecates leaning on the horn-button as being ineffective and vulgar, and looks for some more direct method. With all modesty I believe that in my cannon they have it, for any driver, however absent-minded or comatose, who ignores the impact of a squashy tomato on the back of his neck (rubber balls, for courtesy's sake, having been shot over his head), is surely impervious to sweet reason.

But there are other, though less urgent, justifications for my cannon. Some weeks ago a friend of mine, driving up a lonely stretch of the Great North Road, was interested to see a suit-case, strapped to the carrier of a big car in front, open and disgorge a flowered silk dressing-gown, which hovered in the breeze a little before settling gently over a gate-post. In the car was a girl, alone. My friend, all chivalrous, stepped hard on his battered accelerator, but found he could make little impression on the forty super-charged horses in front.

Should he, he wondered, go back and pick the thing up in the hope of overtaking the girl somewhere at lunch? But the thought of being flung out of one hotel after another up the Great North Road for hawking dressing-gowns, even silk ones, in the restaurant, deterred him, and he decided that pursuit was his only course.

His car had gained a yard or two on the girl's when a silver hand-mirror leaped out of her suit-case and dashed itself to pieces on the road. Another yard nearer and a travelling-clock, a large bottle of scent and one shoe committed *hara-kiri*. My friend, a frugal fellow, was appalled at such waste. Yet another yard gained and other, more intimate, objects began to emerge in rapid succession and frolic merrily in the vacuum behind the girl's car. My friend, a modest fellow, was horrified. But what, lacking my cannon, could he do except indulge in a series of eccentric sequences on his horn, followed by a series of eccentric gestures with his arms, which he realised were open to grave misinterpretation if the occupant of the other car had been at all well brought up? And apparently she had, for, after one anxious appraisal in her mirror of these antics, she trod heavily on the gas and sailed out of my friend's life, scorning such crude attempts at introduction and sartorially, poor girl, very ill-equipped for Scotland. Had my friend been able to project an official rubber ball (such as I recommend for use in cases not so absolutely urgent as to call for ripe fruit, and bearing Mr. HORE-BELISHA's* portrait on one side and Sir STENSON COOKE's† on the other) into her car the moment the suit-case opened, her tears might have been spared.

My cannon, when they adopt it, will make the motor-car an infinitely safer vehicle; but I wish that while they are about improving the means of communication between drivers they would make actual conversations possible and so do away with the melancholy sense of social isolation which afflicts many of us on the King's Highway. Before now I have known the slow approach of two cars on the long straight lonely roads of Suffolk to become so acutely embarrassing that both drivers, while still at a considerable distance, have broken into voluble deaf-and-dumb tic-tac, greatly to the detriment of their steering.

I myself would gladly go to the expense of erecting a small mast above my windscreen on which code-flags could be run up (wireless being presumably too tricky) or a simple semaphore system on the roof, if others would promise to follow suit. In the big cities these days it takes all one's time to keep out of danger, but out in the country what a pleasure it would often be to break the monotony of driving by flapping out a cheerful "I looks towards you!" on the semaphore to an oncoming stranger, and how warming to receive his friendly "I catches your eye!"

Not all the greetings launched by our semaphores, however, would be of such a jovial nature. At present on a long drive the voice soon goes, shouting the plain facts of their origin at the cutters-in and the hullabaloo merchants; but one could joyfully operate a blistering semaphore for hours on end.

* LESLIE HORE-BELISHA, who, as minister of transport (1934) gave his name to the 'Belisha' beacons, drafted a new highway code and inaugurated driving tests for motorists.
† SIR STENSON COOKE, first secretary of the Automobile Association from 1905 to 1942.

"We'll have to let this thing pass. I can't hear
a word you're saying."

WORTHY to serve the most exalted, upon occasions of the utmost circumstance, yet marked by a chaste restraint of line never suggestive of opulence, or arrogance, the Ford V-8 (£16. 10s. Tax) has performance of a measure and refinement making it handsomely worth twice its price of £210. As economical as efficient in its infinite range of duty, it is the car for Britons, the world over, in Coronation Year.

"There Is No Comparison!"

FORD MOTOR COMPANY LIMITED, DAGENHAM, ESSEX, ENGLAND.   LONDON SHOWROOMS. 88 REGENT ST. W.1.

AS OTHERS HEAR US
DRIVING MOTHER IN THE CAR

"NOW, dear, I am quite ready. It's so nice to have a chauffeur. I just want to tell Ellen—"
"D'you want the rug, Mummie?"

"What, darling? No, don't put that parcel on the floor; I'd better take it on my lap. I'm quite ready now. Oh, wait a minute—there was a book to go back to the library."

"It's gone."

"Then let's start, dear. I don't want to be late for my meeting. Just let me see if I've got those papers."

"Wouldn't they be in your bag?"

"Darling, this is the wrong bag. No, it isn't—it's the right one. But the papers aren't there. Yes, they are. No. Yes. Yes—they're all there. Now, darling, we must start. And do remember to be very careful. It's so nice to have a chauffeur."

"Mummie, I do think you ought to speak to Binks about the car. I know it's frightfully old, but really—"

"Old! It's not in the least old. Besides, 1926 was a particularly *good* year—everybody says so. Mind, darling."

"It's all right."

"No, darling, it isn't. You went round that corner a great deal too fast. Suppose some poor woman had been wheeling a pram in the opposite direction in the very middle of the road?"

"Serve her right if she did get run over, if she was in the middle of the road."

"The coroner wouldn't say so. Not that they know what they're talking about, I always think. Why not sound your horn, darling?"

"No really good driver *ever* sounds a horn except in a great emergency."

"Still, dear, you could hardly call yourself a really *good* driver, could you? Though I must say it's nice to have a chauffeur."

"Gosh, Mummie! Look at that bird! I bet anything it's a hawk."

"Very likely, dear, though I must say it looked more like a wood-pigeon to me; but you *must* keep your eyes on the road."

"A wood-pigeon! How could it—?"

"There's a car coming, dear."

"It's all right."

"I think you had better slow down a little. It seems to me to be going much too fast."

"Gosh! it's a beauty."

"Keep your eyes on the road, dear."

"It's all *right* , Mummie. I know how to drive."

"Darling, I'm only trying to help you. Remember the cross-roads, won't you?"

"We're not near them yet."

"I always remember a dreadful accident at the cross-roads, years ago, when people were just beginning to use motor-cars, and a carriage-and-pair got overturned and poor old Mr. Chote was killed. I always think of it whenever I come this way."

"How jolly! I mean to say, really, Mummie, you ought to *try* to get over being so nervous. If it was an aeroplane, now—"

"Don't be silly, dear. And don't you think we ought to go a little faster? I don't want to be late."

"Rather! I only thought you might be nervous."

"Slow down for the cross-roads."

"Is it the next turning, or the one after that?"

"Next on the left, not counting the next."

"The next but one, then?"

"Mind, darling."

"It's absolutely all right, Mummie."

"Doesn't Binks always change gear for the hill here?"

"I shouldn't think so. She's taking it beautifully."

"Still, I don't think it can be very good for the engine. Oh, dear!"

"Was that the turning?"

"I ought to have told you sooner. You'd better go on to the top of the hill and turn round."

"I can back her into the lane."

"No, darling, I think you'd better go to the top of the hill and turn. It'll be much simpler. I think you ought to hoot here. There are children in that cottage. Now, dear, why not turn round here? I'll tell you how far you can go. Not too fast, now. That's perfectly splendid. Now back, very carefully. Go on. Yes, go on. Wait a minute. No, it's all right; I thought there was something coming, but it's all right. Right back, you've got any amount of— Stop! You're nearly in the ditch!"

"But, Mummie, you said—"

"Never mind, dear, we've all got to learn. *Now* we're all right. I think we shall really have to hurry a little or I shall be late. But don't forget the thirty-mile limit."

"We're nowhere near one, are we?"

"We shall be presently. I think the engine's getting rather hot, dear—or is something on fire?"

"I don't think so. Why?"

"Oh, I just smelt a smell of burning. We can have it looked at while I'm at the meeting."

"It's not in the *least* necessary."

"Carefully round the bend, darling. I must say it's very nice to have a chauffeur. And remember, when we get into the town, *look out for the traffic-signals.*"

MISLEADING TERMS.
THE LEVEL CROSSING.

OFFICIALLY
RECOMMEND
WAKEFIELD
PATENT
Castrol

XL IN SUMMER   AA IN WINTER

C · C · WAKEFIELD & CO · LTD · WAKEFIELD HOUSE · CHEAPSIDE · LONDON · E · C · 2

NO PARKING

HE was a little man who wore a pair of postman's trousers, a cap which bore the initials of the local gas company, and a butcher's smock. When I stopped my car outside the "Red Lion" he was leaning against the bar window.

"Can't leave car 'ere, mister," he said, removing a clumsy cherrywood pipe from his mouth.

"But it's doing no harm," I said.

"'Olding up traffic," the little man explained.

"But there isn't any traffic," I protested. Indeed the whole place was as peaceful as any market town which is not having a market day.

"You don't know," he observed judicially. "Might be lots of cars 'long any time. Charrybangs even. Besides," he added, "if bobby catches 'ee leaving it 'e'll lock 'ee up."

I was shaken by this threat. "Then tell me," I said, "what am I supposed to do with it?"

"Ah!" The little man raised his cap and scratched his bald head, as though anxious to do me a personal favour. "This 'ere square," he said, "be Council car-park. I be attendant like."

"So I must leave my car there?"

"That's right, mister."

I got back into the driving-seat and bumped painfully onto the cobbled market square. "There!" I said. "Will that do?"

"Ay," the attendant said, "so be as you be not stopping longer than two hours."

"Rubbish!" I exclaimed impatiently. "I shall be stopping here all afternoon. I've come to see a friend of mine who's staying at the 'Red Lion.'"

"Can't stay 'ere all day, mister," the little man protested. "Two hours is Council's limit."

"But, confound it, man," I cried, "nobody else is going to use your car park! There's room here for a dozen cars, anyway."

"Council's orders, mister," he repeated. "If bobby catches 'ee 'e'll lock 'ee up."

It occurred to me that a stupid country constable and an old-fashioned country Bench might indeed enforce these superfluous restrictions. "Then what *am* I to do with my car?" I asked.

The little man put his hand on my sleeve and pointed to a spot twenty yards down the road. "See that petrol-pump, mister?" he said.

"Yes."

"That's a garridge, that is," he told me in confidence. "Leave car in there long as 'ee likes."

I thanked him, gave him a sixpence, and bumped off over the cobbles again.

The garage was open, so I left my car there and walked back to the "Red Lion". As I reached the door I remembered that I had left in the car a parcel which I had meant to bring with me. I turned and went back to the garage again.

As I entered I saw the little man just leaving: he was pocketing what looked and sounded rather like another sixpence.

I stopped him. "What would your bobby say," I asked, "if he saw you taking that tanner?"

The little man smiled shamelessly.

"Nothing," he said. "'E's my son."

'D'you mind switching off, Sir? She's gaining on me.'

The Beauty of a Rose-Bowl by Tiffany ; the Feel of a Shotgun by Purdey ; the Tone and Touch of a Steinway Pianoforte—only these are comparable with the sheer sensuous delight of driving, even of riding in, a LINCOLN-ZEPHYR. The marvellous refinement, with no power-shortage, of its V-12 engine ; a mind-reading gear-box, which seems to guess your wish of the moment, and grant it ; steering feather-light but rock-sure ; suspension which makes you wonder why less fortunate folk grumble about secondary roads ; and brakes whose efficiency enables you to let the car run freely on open stretches . . . . All these are yours, at ever so little cost, first or last, or in between, in this superlatively fine motor car. Write or ring for a catalogue, now. Name your best date for a road trial which will enable you to apply every test you can devise. In short, let the Lincoln-Zephyr speak for itself.

Double-Entrance Saloon, £480, at Works. Coupé (3-passenger), as illustrated, £455. Limousine, £515. Distributors throughout the British Isles.

LINCOLN CARS LIMITED
(Sole Concessionaires for Lincoln and Lincoln-Zephyr Cars)
GREAT WEST ROAD,
BRENTFORD, MDX.
Telephone: Ealing 4506-7

Lincoln-Zephyr

1937

ROVER
1937
MODELS & PRICES

10 h.p. Saloon	.. .. ..	£248
12 h.p. Saloon	.. .. ..	£285
12 h.p. Sports Saloon	.. ..	£295
14 h.p. Saloon	.. ..	£305
14 h.p. Sports Saloon	.. ..	£315
16 h.p. Saloon	.. ..	£345
16 h.p. Sports Saloon	.. ..	£355
Speed Model Sports Saloon	..	£415

One of Britain's Fine Cars

THE ROVER COMPANY LIMITED, COVENTRY. London Showrooms: Henly's Ltd., Devonshire House, Piccadilly, W.I

CVS—197

MOTOR QUESTIONS

WHAT rushes through the crowded street
With whirring noise and throbbing beat,
Exhaling odours far from sweet?
      The motor-car.

Whose wheels o'er greasy asphalte skim,
Exacting toll of life and limb,
(What is a corpse or so to *him*)?
      The motorist's.

Who flies before the oily gust
Wafted his way through whirling dust,
And hopes the beastly thing will bust?
      The pedestrian.

Who thinks that it is scarcely fair
To have to pay for road repair
While sudden death lies lurking there?
      The ratepayer.

Who as the car goes whizzing past
At such law-breaking stands aghast,
(For forty miles an hour *is* fast)?
      The policeman.

Who hears the case with bland surprise,
And over human frailty sighs,
The while he reads between the lies?
      The magistrate.

THE HAUNTED HOG.

I HAD A LITTLE MOTOR-CAR

ABOUT a mile from Crowsfoot the car, which up till then had been running as sweetly as only a three-year-old can, began to make spluttering noises and altered her gait to a series of convulsive jerks. I slipped the clutch and roared the engine up, which some think beneficial, and I moved the ignition-thing backwards and forwards, but it didn't do any good.

"She's not herself," I said to Margaret.

"Sounds a bit bronchial," said Margaret. "Have you tried moving the ignition-thing backwards and forwards?"

I gave her a look.

"What good would that do?" I said, reasonably enough.

"It only advances and retards the spark; surely you know that?"

Women have such perfectly extraordinary notions about machinery.

At Crowsfoot we found a garage and explained just what the trouble was. "One moment we were humming along," I said "with that smooth, effortless speed which is the hall-mark of the Hodman Family Four, the next she was coughing and spluttering and—well, and spluttering. It was most extraordinary."

"Coughing and spluttering, was she?" said the man.

"Yes," I said. And I added "Fit to bust herself," because these local men are rather apt to try to pooh-pooh one's complaints if one isn't firm with them.

"Sounds like the carb," he said. "Was she spitting?"

I considered the point.

"I don't think I'd call it spitting," said Margaret, who is sometimes just a tiny bit inclined to interfere in matters she really knows nothing about. "Wouldn't you have said it was a sort of hiccup—a kind of interrupted 'hup,' you know? Only with a choke in it?"

"Yes," I said. "Or splutter."

"Might be the ignition," said the man, conceding a point.

I threw my mind back into the immediate past. Had we given him all the information at our disposal? After all, it was hardly fair to expect him to set things to rights unless he had as accurate an account as possible of what had gone wrong.

"There was a kind of golloping noise too," I said at last.

The man looked grave.

"You'd better leave her with me," he said in a kindly tone. "Come back in a R's time and I'll see what I can do."

Crowsfoot Church is unique in some respects and so is the coffee supplied by the Misses Angelica at the "Dainty Tea Rooms", but on the whole we were glad when the R was up. The garage man threw away his apple as we came up, and we stood round the open bonnet while he showed us the sights. Then he started the engine and roared her up. He roared her as loud as any sucking dove—louder in fact. I never heard such a clatter. I judged she would have been doing a hundred-and-sixty on the open road.

"All right?" shouted the man, squeezing another forty out of her.

"Magnificent," I yelled. "Not a splutter."

About five miles out of Crowsfoot the car, which up till then had been running as sweetly as any car will when it has just had its carburettor cleaned out and its plugs looked at, began to make spluttering noises (a sort of hiccup, some would call it, only with a choke in it) and altered her gait to a series of convulsive jerks.

"Sounds like the carb," said Margaret.

I kept quite calm. "Listen," I said. "We must think this thing out. We know there's nothing wrong now with the carburettor or the plugs. Very well, then, what's left? Take the process from the beginning. First of all the petrol has to come from the tank. We ought to make sure it's doing that. The outlet pipe might be blocked—a mouse or something. You see what I'm driving at?"

"Is it easy for mice to get into the petrol-tank?"

"No," I said slowly, "it isn't *easy*, but you can't tell with mice. They get into the tubes of Westinghouse brakes and stop expresses. And that's nothing. I read once of a man who unscrewed the cylinder-head of his car and found a bee buzzing about inside one of the cylinders."

"Heavens!" said Margaret faintly. "We'd better drive to the nearest vet."

Instead, we drove on, bucking horribly, to Snake's End, where I gave the garage proprietor a full and frank account of our difficulties. About a mile on the further side of Crowsfoot, I told him, the car, which was, as he saw, a specimen of the Hodman Family Four (Real Riding Comfort for the Man of Moderate Means), had suddenly started spluttering and, in a word, coughing. At Crowsfoot both carburettor and plugs had received every attention, but five miles further on the spluttering, or yes, as some said, hiccuping, had begun again. It was, I said, most extraordinary.

"My husband thinks there may be a mouse in the petrol-tank," said Margaret.

Of course it is no use talking to garage proprietors about Westinghouse brakes, so I simply let him have his laugh out. When he had finished he said he would have a look round; it might be the points. "Give me half-an-R," he said.

The church at Snake's End is said to be very fine.

About a mile-and-a-half beyond Snake's End the car, which up till then had been running with all the ardour of a Hodman Family Four when it has just been presented with a brand-new set of points, began to—well, you know what it did.

"Oh, dear!" said Margaret.

We crawled painfully on until we came to a blacksmith's forge, and there I descended.

"Have you got a great big sledge-hammer?" I asked.

"R," said the blacksmith.

"Then would you mind catching this—this Hodman Family Four a great big wallop with it?"

He seemed a stupid sort of chap.

"What for?" he said.

"A shilling."

"Orright," he said at last. "Whereabouts d'ya want it?"

I opened the bonnet and laid my finger on the carb.

"Here," I said.

Wallop!

*   *   *   *   *   *   *

Will you believe me when I say that a mouse jumped out of the petrol-tank?

DAME (*seeing the signpost*). "Stop, Jenkins—stop! I think it would be safer to turn back. They may have catapults or something dangerous."

"Here's a Flying Standard V-EIGHT.."

1937

FST V-8

0-50 m.p.h. in 12 seconds

BUY A CAR
MADE IN THE UNITED KINGDOM

Flying Standard
V-EIGHT

"You realise at once that you are handling something that is out of the ordinary . . . . the maximum road speed on high gear is 82 m.p.h. . . . . its performance excels that of many sports cars. The acceleration is particularly good, as from a standstill it can reach a speed of 50 m.p.h. in 12 seconds dead. . . . I liked the car immensely. It has the feeling of a thoroughbred and it behaves as one, and I am sure that this new model will prove a tremendous success."

Sir Malcolm Campbell sums up in "The Field."

£349
EX WORKS

DETAILS OF THIS AMAZING CAR FROM— **THE STANDARD MOTOR CO. LTD., CANLEY, COVENTRY**
WEST END SHOWROOMS— **"STANDARD CARS," 37 DAVIES ST., GROSVENOR SQ., LONDON, W.1.**

1938

The Wolseley 25-h.p. Limousine . . . £775.
Dunlops, Triplex and Jackalls, of course . . .
Other models from £245.

Entourage

TO A WOMAN with social activities a car represents something far more than a means of transportation. She may be attracted by the luxurious comfort and spaciousness of a Wolseley Limousine — the soothing quietness of its well-lighted, unobtrusively ventilated interior — its strong, silent power. But subconsciously it will mean a great deal more to her. Its long, graceful and distinguished appearance must seem a natural setting for her position in life — a lengthened reflection of the taste and beauty of her home. When you consider a Wolseley Limousine in that light, you realise that its ownership would be most apt in your own case. . . .

Buy Wisely – Buy WOLSELEY

Wolseley Motors Ltd., Ward End, Birmingham 8.   London Distributors : Eustace Watkins Ltd., Berkeley St., W.1. Sole Exporters : M.I.E. Ltd., Cowley, Oxford, Eng.

A CURE FOR BAD DRIVING

IT is practically impossible to glance at any newspaper – *The Times* included – without seeing something about Bad Driving. If it doesn't form the subject of an article, there are sure to be several letters to the editor containing lurid accounts of the writers' hairbreadth escapes. And all the people who can't be bothered to write to the papers about it employ it as a fool-proof topic of conversation in drawing-rooms, clubs, at parties and, in fact, everywhere. Even if they don't drive they are certain to have a great many friends and relations who do, and there's nothing that gives them more pleasure than to tell you exactly how these friends and relations have been run into, concussed and ditched. Bad Drivers again.

Roughly speaking there is one Bad Driver to twenty good (or, at any rate, well-meaning) ones; but what is written or spoken about the remaining nineteen? Next to nothing.

These well-behaved motorists who spend their time not running over wool-gathering pedestrians, getting out of the way of the pushers, straining their eyes to see invisible cyclists after dark, waiting for the *green* light at crossings and parking not more than six inches from the kerb, are merely taken for granted; but this state of affairs, as every intelligent man, woman and child will at once see, is all wrong, for it is the skill and prowess of the well-behaved nineteen which should be broadcast throughout the country.

With the idea of bringing this about, I have thought out a scheme which, if carried out universally, would revolutionise motoring. There are of course many more by-passes to be explored and corners left unturned, but the broad outlines are as follows: –

I – THE PRESS

Every time you read a letter in a newspaper bringing to notice an example of Bad Driving, immediately send in another giving an example of Good Driving. For instance, suppose you see this: –

"SIR, – While proceeding at 30 m.p.h. along the Oxford-Cheltenham road, a large car endeavoured to overtake me round a bend. As it drew level a motor-coach came into view, causing the driver of the saloon, in order to avoid a head-on crash, to force me off the road. I managed to come to rest in some stinging-nettles, but the other car charged the hedge, struck a tree, rebounded back on to the road, turned round twice and finally came to rest beside me. By a miracle no one was hurt; but imagine my utter amazement when the fellow approached me with clenched fists, saying, '*How dare you*, Sir?' – INDIGNANT, *Leamington Spa*,"

your counter-attack should be something like this –

"SIR, – The following incident may be of interest to your readers. While motoring on the Great West Road last Thursday I found myself behind a slower car. There was nothing coming for as far as I could see – a quarter-of-a-mile – so I sounded my horn gently. The driver of the leading car instantly drew in to his left, slackened his pace slightly and courteously waved me on. As I passed him I touched my hat, receiving in reply an extremely pleasant smile. – SATISFIED, *Windsor.*"

You see the idea? If the thing got going on a large scale we should soon have the reputation of being the best drivers in the world.

II – PARKING

Of course there are certain people who never will be able to park a car anywhere but in the middle of the road at important bus-stops; but there are many thousands of others who daily worm their way neatly and unobtrusively into small gaps without knocking over street musicians, old women selling matches and bicycles propped delicately against the kerb. But do these skilled "manœuvrers" ever have their backs patted? No. Very Well, then, descend on these expert parkers and congratulate them on their work. Go up to them, shake them warmly by the hand and use any of the following: –

    (1) "Well parked, Sir!"
    (2) "What accuracy!"
    (3) "What style!"
    (4) "Nicely judged, Sir!"

LETTERS TO OFFICIALDOM
IX— *Re* Driving Test

To the Minister of Transport, The Ministry of Transport, Whitehall Gardens, London S.W.1.

DEAR SIR,—I am not one to lodge complaints or cavil at my lot without due cause, but this does not apply to my wife. I feel very strongly about any lot of my wife's and I think you should know this. She has been married to me now for many years; I started teaching her to drive in January, 1935, and now one of your official examiners has failed her for the fourth time. You may think this a reflection on my wife's ability, but when you have heard the facts you will realise that your examiner at Rumborough has treated her exceedingly unjustly.

I readily concede that in the first three tests my wife *did* lapse from that degree of absolute proficiency she had attained with me when driving up and down a country lane. This was because your examiner refused to take her to this same lane, and made her drive in traffic. My wife was not used to traffic and pedestrians, though she has had experience with cows in the lane I refer to—and cows take a lot of understanding, though perhaps not quite as much as pedestrians. Anyway in the first test my wife mistook the gear-lever for the hand-brake and reversed the car into a milk-float and, seeing the spilt milk, thought she had hit a cow until she remembered where she was (Earl's Court Road).

In the second test she inadvertently switched the traffic-indicator to the left when about to turn to the right, realised her mistake, quickly extended her right arm, sounded the horn with her other hand, and then, having no hand free with which to steer, was forced to go straight on. This might not have mattered, but a bus-driver rudely told her to "bloomin' well try Morse instead of semaphoring," and this upset her so much that she could not go on. In the third test, six months later, she drove head-on into a pillar-box, overturning it. Luckily it was one of the very old V.R. (Victoria Rex) ones, and so far from being disconcerted my wife, whose name is Victoria, wittily observed, "Victoria wrecks (Rex) the pillar-box!" Of course the joke was lost on the examiner and the policeman because they did not know my wife's name was Victoria. I doubt too if they knew Latin.

I agree then that there was some excuse for my wife failing in these three tests, which were held in London. It is about the fourth test, held down here in Wiltshire, that I am writing to complain. I may say that one of the reasons why we left London was to enable my wife to be examined in a country lane, but your examiner in Rumborough would not hear of this. He insisted on her going into Rumborough, which is a very busy town, and began by asking her to drive round the square.

My wife, accustomed by now to the traps set by your examiners, instantly said she couldn't do it. When pressed, she asked if he would take full responsibility, and he said he would. This is definite. Your examiner said he would take full responsibility, so my wife had no alternative but to obey. She accordingly drove round the square, anti-clockwise, in the manner shown in the diagram below.

As you can see, she kept as close as possible to the corners of the square A-B-C-D, and just managed to keep off the pavements E-F-G-H. At K she unfortunately tipped over an errand-boy's bicycle standing against the kerb, but this was her only mishap—though some slight disorganisation of the traffic occurred on the London-Bath road, which passes through the square, while she was executing the manœuvre.

Imagine her chagrin therefore when, having completed the circle and pulled up, she was told by your examiner that *until she had learnt the first rule of the road—to keep to the left—she could not enter again for the test.* I wonder, Sir, did you ever hear of such a trick? You have only to look at the diagram to see that *no one* could drive *round* the square without impinging on the outer pavements. I tried it myself after dark last evening, and nearly drove right into the cinema (N on diagram).

Please let me know if, after this experience, my wife need enter for the test again.

Yours faithfully, CHAS. CURSETT

P.S.—I forgot to say that s in the diagram is the statue of Roger, Lord Rum, the great reformer. He started reforming at Rum Hall by the river (the Rum), hence his title (Lord Rum).

THE TYRE OF THE CENTURY

G-100
ALL-WEATHER

NEW COMPRESSION BUILT TREAD

Conventional Tyre
When inflated all portions expand — tread S-T-R-E-T-C-H-E-S — which makes it easy to cut or bruise.

G-100 Uninflated
Note that the new G-100, when uninflated, is flat-sided, higher than it is wide — a new construction principle.

G-100 Inflated
Sidewalls expand — tread contracts. Compressed rubber wears longer, resists cuts — result 33% longer life.

33% MORE MILEAGE

The new G-100 is named in honour of the 100th Anniversary of Charles Goodyear's discovery of vulcanization. But it merits its title—"The Tyre of the Century" by its amazing performance: 33% longer wear, increased stability, greater riding comfort and non-skid safety. A revolutionary new principle of construction — the "Compression Built" Tread, is responsible for this new standard of tyre performance at no extra cost. Ask your dealer to show you G-100 — the tyre of the Century.

GOODYEAR
FACTORY AT WOLVERHAMPTON

1939

For going places and seeing things in comfort—

THE CAR FOR A STAR
Miss Carol Goodner, the well-known actress, caught by the camera in an Austin '14' Goodwood at Heston.

EYX 770

The AUSTIN FOURTEEN

The speed, the economy, the sensible smartness of the Austin Fourteen make an immediate appeal to a woman. Here is a car she can drive at seventy miles an hour—in comfort and in safety. A car she can weave in and out of traffic—with confidence and ease. A car she can be proud to be seen in at the smartest places. The Austin Fourteen has taken "firsts" at coachwork competitions again and again. And besides being lovely to look at it's delightful to drive.

The big comfortable seats, the adjustable steering, the accessible controls and ample luggage accommodation are a few of the many things which make an Austin Fourteen such a sound investment from a woman's point of view.

GOODWOOD Fixed-Head Saloon	**£235**
GOODWOOD SALOON	**£245**
GOODWOOD CABRIOLET	**£252**

(at works)
Jackall Jacks £5.10.0. extra.

Models can be seen at any Austin Dealer's or at Austin's London Showrooms, 479 Oxford Street, W.1. Read the "Austin Magazine," 4d. every month.

INVEST IN AN AUSTIN 'FOURTEEN'

THE AUSTIN MOTOR COMPANY LIMITED, LONGBRIDGE, BIRMINGHAM

5.D.67

MOTOR CAR · ACTERISTICS
(By an Old Whip)

JERKING and jolting,
Bursting and bolting,
Smelling and steaming,
Shrieking and screaming,
Snorting and shaking,
Quivering, quaking,
Skidding and slipping,
Twisting and tripping,
Bumping and bounding,
Puffing and pounding,
Rolling and rumbling,
Thumping and tumbling.
Such I've a notion,
Motor-car motion.

"Just because we are English you needn't think my sister and I won't make a fuss about this."